CONCEPT CARS

CONCEPT CARS

Jonathan Wood

OO5799

This is a Parragon Book

© Parragon 1997

Parragon

Units 13-17, Avonbridge Trading Estate,

Atlantic Road, Avonmouth,

Bristol BS11 9QD

Designed, produced and packaged by

Touchstone, Old Chapel Studio,

Plain Road, Marden, Tonbridge,

Kent TN12 9LS, United Kingdom

Edited by Philip de Ste. Croix

ISBN 0-75252-084-9

Printed in Italy

Page 1: Ford's 435bhp Indigo, effectively a two-seater Formula 1 car with carbon-fibre body and mid-located, quad cam, V12 engine, announced at the 1996 Detroit Show. Page 2: From top left clockwise: Chrysler's 1997 Jeep Icon, bird's eye view of 1993 Mercedes-Benz F100, 1995 Ford Synergy 2010, where's the steering wheel? Impression of Mercedes-Benz's 1996 F200. Title page: 1997 Alfa Romeo Scighera by Ital Design unveiled at the 1997 Geneva Show. Above: Pininfarina's 1996 Fiat-based mini Multi Purpose Vehicles: Sing (left) and Song.

Photographic credits

All pictures are courtesy of the relevant manufacturers and styling houses with the exception of the following:

Neill Bruce Motoring Photolibrary: 22, 23 (main), 23 (inset), 32-33, 40 (top), 57 (below), 58-59, 82 (top), 82 (below).

Haymarket Publishing: 10, 11 (below), 34-35, 46-47.

David Hodges: 16-17.

Ludvigsen Library: 8-9, 12-13.

Magna Press: 28-29.

Andrew Morland: 6 (top).

John Ward: 11 (top).

Picture research by **Neill Bruce**

Contents

Introduction

A visit to a motor show can be an enthralling experience for the car buff and interested spectator alike. But the vehicles that often attract the largest crowds are not always the latest production models.

They are the visually stunning, colourful and sometimes zany concept cars for which the stylist and engineer have been given a free rein, untrammelled by the restrictions of price and the demands of the manufacturing process.

The concept car, a name that was not coined until the 1980s, is really as old as the motor car itself, and the shows where cars are exhibited.

The automobile was born in Germany in 1886, but in the early years car makers were usually only responsible for their vehicle's mechanicals. Bodywork was invariably farmed out to a coachbuilder who previously had built horsedrawn carriages.

Customers could order their car bodies in much the same way that they might a new suit, and this meant that handcrafted coachwork was produced in an infinite number of lines and styles.

The place where coach-builders sought to display their latest products, often visually extravagant one-offs, was the shop window of an international motor show, the first of which was held in Berlin in 1897.

But the demise of the coachbuilt body in the 1920s, and its replacement on mass-produced models by the pressed steel one, meant that manufacturers were able to exercise far greater control over the appearance of their cars than hitherto.

Above: The Swiss-based Rinspeed's Formula 1 retro Mono Ego, by French fashion designer, Jean Charles de Castelbajac, wowed the punters at Geneva '97. Top speed was an eye watering 257km/h (160mph).

In America, General Motors established its Art and Colour section in 1927 under the direction of the formidable designer Harley Earl. This department exercised a profound influence on the styling of GM's bevy of makes. In 1939 Earl completed the Buick-based Y-Job that, in retrospect, can be regarded as the first concept car. Long, low and audacious, it allowed him to 'think aloud' and incorporate in a single vehicle many of his

Left: Renault's 1997 four-wheel-drive concept Pangea. 'Whole of the Earth' in Greek, a gas turbine/electric hybrid with a trailer containing the power unit and liquid petroleum gas tank.

predictions for the future, some of which did eventually reach the production line.

Motorama

The Y-Job paved the way for General Motors' own motor show, the Motorama, which was first staged in 1950. It endured until 1961. In the era of the tailfin, aircraft influences and excesses of chromium plate, GM was able to show to the public the ideas that it was considering, and was able to gauge their reaction in turn to what were then known as dream cars.

The demise of the Motorama happily did not spell the end for such vehicles. It meant instead that the Corporation fell in line with the other car makers and displayed them at motor shows. There manufacturers could be guaranteed the maximum of publicity and exposure.

Over the years America had seen the motor car grow virtually unchecked in size until the industry was hit by the oil price rises of the 1970s, triggered by the 1973 Arab/Israeli War.

As a result, a trend to smaller, more economical cars took hold and the science of aerodynamics began once again to influence the design of the bodywork of family models. To prepare the public for this shift in emphasis, these wind-cheating lines first appeared on concept cars.

Many vehicles had tended, up to this period, to highlight stylistic and interior

Above: Rover's surprise at Geneva '97 was its Mini concept Spiritual, not with front-wheel-drive but a three-cylinder, in-line engine tucked out of the way beneath the rear seat.

Below: The Peugeot 605-based Pininfarina Nautilus, also featured at Geneva 1997, was the work of former General Motors stylist Ken Okuyama. It is unlikely to enter production.

refinements. But the advent of the 1980s saw a growing awareness of the impact of the motor car on the environment. In consequence alternative power sources began to feature as important elements of concept cars. There was nothing new in this, gas turbines and the Wankel engine had appeared years before, but had been sidelined.

Electrically Powered Cars

Recently car makers have been attracted to the electrically powered car because it does not produce harmful emissions, even if the power stations that generate the electricity sometimes do.

The non-polluting, electrically powered vehicle and the diesel or petrol/electric hybrid thus figure significantly in the current crop of concept cars.

Of one thing we can be certain. Whatever power source is chosen for the 21st century automobile, the concept car will feature it first!

General Motors Y-Job 1939

Universally regarded as the first of the concept cars, the Y-Job marked a recognition by the mighty General Motors corporation of the increasing importance of styling in the evolution of its stable of makes.

A 1937 Buick chassis was prepared and extended to nearly 6096mm (20ft) in length by the division's chief engineer, Charles Chayne, and his team. Art and Colour's Harley Earl then proceeded to fit it with a two-seater roadster body that bristled with new concepts and initiatives.

The Y's long, low look was accentuated by the use of longitudinal mouldings on the front and rear wings and, in the former case, the wing line was extended for the first time into the front door panels. Yet more daringly the grille featured vertical, rather than the customary horizontal, bars.

The front end of the car pointed the way forward as the wings, although still identifiable, were beginning to merge with the bonnet line. A further Earl initiative, that gave the nose and its immediate surround a smooth, sculptured quality, was the use of concealed headlamps in the manner of the Cord 810 of 1935.

The bonnet was surmounted by what the press release accompanying the car's launch described as a 'machine-gun sight' mascot that was fitted in refined form to all Buicks produced between 1946 and 1958.

Further innovations were the use of flush-fitting door handles, a convertible top that disappeared beneath a metal

Below: The low, innovative Buick-based 1939 Y-Job in its post 1947 form, with concealed headlamps, lack of running boards and flush fitting door handles. Its full impact would not be felt until after the Second World War.

deck and electrically operated windows. There were no running boards, but these had been also absent from the in-house Cadillac's Series 60 Special of 1938.

The Car of the Future

The Y-Job, completed late in 1939, was unveiled by GM in the spring of 1940 when it was promptly hailed as the 'Car of the Future'. But America's involvement, from December 1941, in the Second World War meant that the car was set aside, although the distinctive radiator grille found its way on to the few 1942-model-year Buicks produced before the attack on Pearl Harbor.

Harley Earl used the Y-Job as his personal transport throughout the war. It subsequently underwent modest modifications, one of which involved concealing the rear wheels beneath spats which extended the mouldings along the length of the wing.

The car certainly anticipated the shape of post-war cars with their emphasis on horizontals, and the 1950s' crop of what were then collectively known as dream cars.

Fortunately General Motors retained this historic vehicle, and in the 1970s presented it to the Henry Ford Museum at Dearborn, Michigan. There the Y-Job keeps company with the LeSabre roadster, its 1951 successor.

Above: The Y's electrically powered hood was concealed by this metal deck. The 1938 date refers to the car's conception, not its completion.

Top: The dashboard is not the original unit but is a 1949 Buick-style one which the car still retains.

Triumph TRX 1950

In 1944 Standard bought the moribund Triumph company with a view to transforming it into a sporting marque. This enterprise began a little uncertainly with the Roadster of 1946, best remembered for its archaic dickey seat.

Then in 1947 Standard's managing director, Sir John Black, asked his chief stylist, Walter Belgrove, to design a body for a new sporting Triumph. What was named the Roadster TRX took a protracted three years to evolve; the finished product was eventually unveiled at the 1950 London Motor Show.

Built on a slightly lengthened Standard Vanguard chassis, the car was an uneasy mixture of European and American themes with full-width bodywork in the Italian manner, although the radiator grille was conceived more in the trans-Atlantic idiom.

Power Assistance

The concealed headlamps revealed echoes of Harley Earl's Y-Job but on the Triumph their covers were electrically operated. Power assistance was also applied to electrically activated hydraulics that were used to adjust the bench-type seat, raise the hood and activate the built-in jacks. These devices operated independently of the engine and could thus be used when it was not running.

As far as the TRX's styling was concerned, Belgrove attempted to introduce some family resemblance to the Vanguard saloon. The car was powered by a twin-carburettored version of its 2 litre engine and the bonnet could be opened from either side to gain access to the four-cylinder unit.

Standard forsook traditional coachbuilding methods, in which an ash frame was clad in hand-formed panels, when the Triumph was designed. Instead, the Roadster's stubby, bulbous body was made of double-skinned aluminium.

The car could be used on the road although when *The Autocar's* representative came to drive the Roadster, he was alarmed to find that 'there was a slight suggestion of slow pitching' which only resolved itself once a passenger was on board . . .

Below: John Ward, who owns both surviving TRXs, at the wheel of one of them; the third car caught fire and was destroyed. They were built by Helliwells of Walsall, Staffordshire. But Triumph's Standard owners decided not to proceed and opted for the TR2.

Left: Halfway house between a tourer and sports car, the TRX of 1950 represented the first steps in Triumph's evolution into a sporting make. The chassis and engine were courtesy of the Standard Vanguard. The small badge just ahead of the base of the front wing is a B, for stylist Walter Belgrove, that echoed the Pinin Farina motif.

Below: The TRX's concealed headlamps were inspired by the American Cord 810. Semaphore indicators were not fitted, instead flashing units were used although they were not legal in Britain. A column gear change and bench front seat meant that three occupants could be accommodated.

The TRX was also displayed at the 1950 Paris show, then later at the following year's Geneva event and could be seen in the Transport Hall of the 1951 Festival of Britain.

Costly Concept

The long gestation period unfortunately meant that the car's lines had begun to date and, perhaps wisely, Standard decided not to continue with what had proved a complicated and costly concept. Just three examples of the TRX were built, of which two survive.

Instead Walter Belgrove went on to essay the lines of the far cheaper and more practical TR2 that appeared at the 1952 London Motor Show. It was to be the first of a long running and well regarded sports-car line.

General Motors LeSabre 1951

In America the concept car, or the dream car as it was then known, took a dramatic leap forward in 1951 when General Motors unveiled Harley Earl's sensational and outrageous Le Sabre.

Like the Y-Job, it was built on a Buick chassis which was cloaked with a two-door convertible aluminium body a

Below: LeSabre's experimental 215 cid (3.5 litre), supercharged, V8 engine that developed an amazing 335bhp . . .

mere 914mm (3ft) high. The design audaciously united elements closely associated with a jet fighter and more orthodox automotive themes.

The post-war years had witnessed the arrival of the jet age and the LeSabre took its name from North American Aviation's F-86 Sabre that was the US Air Force's first swept-wing jet fighter.

Jet Engine-Inspired

Like the aircraft, the front of the car was dominated by a jet engine-inspired air intake. This was masked by a horizontal barred grille which unobtrusively incorporated on its reverse side

the car's headlamps. It was automatically rotated to bring them into use.

The aeronautical theme was reinforced at the back of the car by the presence of a stylized outlet duct reminiscent of a jet's. Each tail fin concealed a 90-litre (20-gallon) aircraft-type rubberized fuel tank: one contained methanol and the other petrol. This volatile cocktail was required to

fuel the car's experimental, high-compression, supercharged, 215cid (3533cc), aluminium V8 engine. A de Dion rear axle was employed.

A wraparound windscreen was a further innovation but this created plenty of technical headaches for the Lilley-Owens-Ford company which made it. Happily the firm persevered and it went on to become the largest supplier of such 'screens to the industry.

Aircraft Instrumentation

Instrumentation had more in common with an aircraft than a car and this influence was reflected in the dials that included a tachometer, compass and altimeter.

Electric motors were used to adjust the seats, which incorporated thermostatically activated seat warmers. These were based on the principles developed for electrically warmed flying suits.

Doors were also secured by electrical catches and the roof was similarly activated. It automatically closed at the first few drops of rain.

LeSabre was shown in model form in 1949, was unveiled in 1951, and, together with its Buick-based XP-300 stablemate, was one of the stars of General Motors' 1953 Motorama.

Thereafter Harley Earl used the car as his personal transport for some years and it was often seen in the car parks

of the Grosse Pointe country clubs that he patronized. He even loaned it to General Eisenhower when he was NATO commander in Paris. Goodness knows what the French thought of the Gallic-sounding LeSabre!

Above: GM's styling guru, Harley Earl, in the foreground with Buick's general manager Ivan Wiles at the wheel of LeSabre, with chief engineer Charles Chayne as passenger. Behind is Paul Garnett head of General Motors PR.
Below: The aircraft-style dashboard.

Bertone BAT 1953/55

Below: First of the series, BAT 5 of 1953, built on the Alfa Romeo 1900 Sprint chassis. Entry was fairly easy with bucket seats fitted, although there is only about 50mm (2in) headroom!

F ew would argue that the most memorable contribution made by American designers to the appearance of the road car was the tail fin. Its use there was essentially decorative but the Europeans also recognized that the fin could provide a positive aid to a vehicle's aerodynamic efficiency and roadholding.

This philosophy was memorably embodied in Italy by Bertone's BAT cars, a trio of coupés of such visual extravagance that they would not have looked out of place in the garage of the great Batman himself!

Flying Saucer

After the war the Italian Alfa Romeo company, hitherto a manufacturer of exclusive sports cars, joined the ranks of the mass producers with its 1900 model of 1950. A more potent Sprint version followed in 1951.

Alfa Romeo was intent on improving the aerodynamics of its bodies and to this end, in 1952, it had essayed an experimental streamlined version of the 1900. The

Below: The full complement of BATs, left to right, 5, 7 and 9. Tail fins were introduced to eliminate the tendency of the rear ends to lift at high speed.

Below right: BAT 7 was the most visually extravagant of the trio. The slots equalized air pressure on the inner and outer surfaces of the fins.

resulting Disco Volante (Flying Saucer) was a stylistically adventurous concept, but it proved to be a flawed one, and the company then turned to the Turin styling and coachbuilding house of Bertone for its ideas.

Bat-mobile

The result was the BAT series, which stood for Berlina Aerodinamica Tecnica, the work of Bertone's stylist, graduate engineer Franco Scaglione.This talented Florentine had joined the firm in 1951 and was well versed in the science of aerodynamics.

One of the shortcomings of the Disco Volante's body was that it tended to concentrate air pressure towards the front of the car and away from the driven wheels at the rear.

Unfortunately, roadholding suffered accordingly.

The 1900 Sprint-based BAT 5 coupé, that appeared in mid-1953, was created with the express intention of redressing this balance by transferring airflow back towards the rear of the car. For this reason the BAT's rear wings were its most visually dramatic feature. These began at the line of the deeply curved windscreen and progressively increased in height as they reached the rear of the car.

Above: BAT 9, the last of the series, retained the Alfa Romeo radiator and almost conventional headlamps.

BAT 5, with an impressive drag coefficient (Cd) of 0.23, was followed in 1954 by the even more extravagant BAT 7, which was displayed at that year's Turin Motor Show. With an improved Cd of 0.19 it featured even higher curvilinear wings that rose to the height of the car's teardrop-shaped cockpit. Finally, at the 1955 event, the less radical BAT 9 appeared.

Just how successful these concepts were must remain open to question, but they did raise the small Bertone company's international profile. The BATs also paved the way for lucrative contracts with Alfa Romeo in the form of a coupé body for the lovely Giulietta SS of 1957, and the long-running Guilia line of 1966-77 vintage.

Ford Mustang 1962

meant that Bordinat was able to design a low roadster body with a chisel-shaped nose. Its clean lines were in striking contrast to the befinned and chromed excesses of the previous decade.

While many concept cars have pointed the way towards production models, others have not. One vehicle that falls decisively into the latter category is Ford's Mustang I, which can be seen as the first tentative step along a road which eventually led to the arrival of the definitive best-selling Mustang in 1964.

This car was the brainchild of Lee Iacocca, newly appointed chairman of the company's Ford Division, who recognized that the post-war baby boom was due to reach adulthood in the 1960s. Market research told him that this new youthful generation would instantly respond to a sporty car, in fact just the type of vehicle that Ford was *not* building.

Total Performance

Iacocca argued that having bought such a model, customers would invariably remain loyal to the marque for the rest of their purchasing lives. It was for such hard-nosed marketing reasons that Ford introduced its so-called Total Performance programme.

Mustang I represented the starting point of this shift in corporate emphasis, although, paradoxically, it was a small car by American standards and very European in concept.

This was because Roy Lunn, one of the key players in the project, was an Englishman who had emigrated to America in 1958 to become head of the company's advanced engineering department.

There, he and fellow engineer, Frank Theyleg, had in 1959 conceived the idea of taking the compact V4 engine created in the US for Ford Germany's Taunus 12M saloon, and mid-locating it in a sports car. It was an approach that would be applied to Mustang I.

Lunn became the project's product planner, and the car was engineered by Herb Misch, latterly of Studebaker, and styled by veteran Ford designer Gene Bordinat.

Mid-Engined

An uncompromising two-seater, the 1.9 litre Ford V4 engine was mounted amidships and secured in a multi-tubular frame. Suspension, unusually for an American automobile, was all independent.

The engine's position

The Mustang I was well received by the crowds at its debut at the US Grand Prix of October 1962, and the company produced a second non-running example for display at motor shows.

But Ford then decided not to continue with such a sophisticated design that, in truth, did not lend itself to mass production. Instead it proceeded with its sporty, conventionally engined, four-seater Mustang II of 1963 that emerged as the definitive model in the following year. It went on to become one of the fastest-selling cars in the history of the American automobile.

Below: Mustang I, the mid-engined V4 open two-seater, did not lend itself to mass-production, and so, bore no resemblance to the production car which was conventionally engineered. It was European in concept and, happily, survives in the Henry Ford Museum.

Mercedes-Benz CIII 1969

In 1964 the German NSU concern introduced the Spyder, the world's first Wankel-engined production car. For the next 15 or so years, many of the world's leading motor manufacturers toyed with this rotary power unit until it finally was dropped by an industry that, by the late 1970s, was turning towards smaller and less polluting cars.

One of the many companies that experimented with the concept was Mercedes-Benz, and its ingenious mid-engined CIII coupé appeared in 1969. The triple rotor, fuel-injected power unit, displacing the equivalent of 3.6 litres, had the distinction of being the largest capacity Wankel engine of its day and it endowed this sleek coupé with a top speed of 265km/h (165mph).

Gull-Wing Doors

The mid-location of the power unit meant that the car had an aerodynamically efficient nose, while the two-seater, glass-fibre bodywork incorporated Mercedes-Benz's legendary gull-wing doors. These had been made famous by the 300SL coupé of 1954-57 vintage.

Despite rumours that the company would produce a run of 50 cars, in reality only a handful were built, one of which subsequently appeared at the

Below: The mid- (Wankel) engined CIII, as revised in 1970. Note the cooling grilles for the power unit. The distinctive rear end 'flying buttresses' were retained for aerodynamic reasons.

wake of the 1973-4 oil price rise, triggered by the Arab/Israeli war. In addition the problem of emissions, particularly on the all-important American market, had assumed critical significance and most manufacturers consequently sidelined the thirsty, polluting Wankel. Mercedes-Benz was one of them.

However, the concept formed the basis of the CIII/III record-breaking coupé of 1976 which sported a five-cylinder turbocharged diesel fitted in place of the rotary unit. A further development of 1979, the CIII/IV, powered by a 500bhp turbocharged V8 engine, lapped the Nardo circuit in Italy at over 402km/h (250mph), so breaking the world's old established closed-course speed record.

1970 Geneva Motor Show. This featured revised bodywork incorporating changes to the nose and tail made with a view to improving the driver's rear visibility.

cheaper to build and was also more compact.

But on the debit side was heavier petrol and oil consumption, which produced more emissions, and, above

all, undue wear on the seals on the tips of the triangular rotor at the unit's heart.

At this time, the world was turning to smaller-capacity, more economical cars in the

Rotary Engine

Less outwardly apparent was the fact that the engine was now a four-rotor unit and the equivalent of 4.8 litres in capacity. Top speed was a claimed 299km/h (186mph).

The appeal of a rotary engine such as the Wankel was compelling. It offered the driver smooth, turbine-like power and was more mechanically efficient than a conventional reciprocating engine. It accordingly used fewer components, was

Bertone Stratos 1970

The phenomenally successful Lancia Stratos has the distinction of being the only example of a car that was specifically designed for rallying. Usually manufacturers opted for extensively modified road models as their rally entrants.

The Stratos is also significant for having begun life as a Bertone styling exercise that was in a state of constant evolution between the years of 1968 and 1971.

In 1967 Alfa Romeo had introduced the exclusive 2 litre, mid-V8-engined Stradale coupé based on its sports-racing Type 33. The company soon made the chassis available to Pininfarina, Bertone and Ital Design, and each displayed their own versions.

The starting point for the Stratos was Bertone's interpretation, titled Carabo, that proved to be the sensation of the 1968 Paris Motor Show.

Beetle Drive

Named after the carabus beetle, it was a daring wedge-shaped concept. The doors ingeniously opened upwards rather like a mollusc opening its shell.

This car was the work of Bertone's young stylist, Marcello Gandini, later responsible for the lines of the Lamborghini Muira and even more sensational Countach, both of which had their engines amidships.

Using the Carabo as his starting point, Gandini went on to produce an extraordinary wedge-shaped creation. The mid-engined configuration, with a Lancia Fulvia HF V4 unit mounted in-line, was once again adopted. Unusually there was a single front door that hinged at the roof.

Stratospheric Styling

On seeing this car in the making, a Bertone employee is reputed to have exclaimed that the vehicle looked as though it had come from the stratosphere, from which the Stratos name evolved.

It was displayed to great acclaim at the 1970 Turin Motor Show. Impractical as the concept was, Lancia's competition manager, Cesare

Below: Marcello Gandini's mid- (Fulvia) engined Bertone Stratos HF of 1970 in which the lines of the legendary Lancia rally car of the same name are already visible. It finally appeared in 1974.

Florio, believed that it could evolve into a rally car. In March 1971, Bertone was given approval to proceed with the prestigious project.

At that year's Turin Show, Bertone unveiled its Stratos HF, a more practical offering than the 1970 car. It retained the vitality of the original but now possessed two conventionally located doors. It also differed from the previous year's concept in being powered by a transversely mounted 2.4 litre V6 engine from the in-house Ferrari Dino 246.

Further body refinements followed before the definitive Stratos appeared in 1974.

Above: Entry to this sensational two-seater was through the single-hinged door, which doubled as a windscreen. Right: The louvres in the engine cover featured a distinctive triangular theme. Beneath was a 1.6 litre V4 unit.

Bertone was awarded the body contract for a vehicle that used a robust steel substructure and glass-fibre body panels.

The Stratos was soon sweeping all before it and Lancia won the World Rally Championship in 1975 and 1976. To obtain homologation the Stratos also had to be offered as a road car and just 492 examples of this stubby masterpiece were built.

Aston Martin Bulldog 1980

Since 1987 Aston Martin has been positioned safely within Ford's corporate corral. Yet only twelve years before, in 1975, it had been rescued from bankruptcy by a consortium headed by American company doctor, Peter Sprague, and British entrepreneur, Alan Curtis.

To commemorate this ongoing renaissance and to publicize a newly created external engineering facility, in 1980 the firm unveiled the unique mid-engined Bulldog. It was a concept that enjoyed a mixed reception from the press but generated worldwide publicity for the revitalized company.

Supercar

Chairman Curtis maintained that the Bulldog had been created to show 'that Aston Martin can build the ultimate roadgoing supercar.' Its low, angular, wedge-shaped body was the work of William Towns who had already styled the firm's V8 coupé and futuristic Lagonda saloon.

The car had a protracted gestation. Work began in 1977 under engineering manager, Mike Loasby, but when he left to join the DeLorean operation in Northern Ireland late in 1978, the job was briefly set to one side.

Reactivated early in 1979 under projects manager, Keith

Martin, and development engineer, Keith Hallam, it was completed in little over a year. The left-hand-drive Bulldog was finally unleashed on the motoring press in April 1980.

British Bulldog

The Britishness of the name seemed appropriate. It had come about because the car

had begun life as DP (for Development Project) K.901. This was shortened to Canine, and so in turn it became Bulldog. The area of Aston Martin's Newport Pagnell factory where the car ultimately took shape was known, inevitably, as The Kennel.

Unduly wide, angular and low, the Bulldog was just 1092mm (43in) high, and possessed a drag coefficient of 0.34. Massive hydraulically

Below: The Bulldog's gull-wing doors were hydraulically-operated. Their lower portions incorporated the sills.

activated gull-wing doors were fitted and operated by buttons contained under lockable hatches.

Some commentators responded positively to a shape that was totally devoid of decorative features, while others found it excessively bland. Of one thing both parties were agreed: the Bulldog looked like nothing else.

Unlike Aston Martin's road cars which were front-engined, the 5.3 litre V8, twin-turbocharged in the Bulldog, was mid-located. A tubular chassis was employed with a

de Dion rear axle and conventional coils and wishbones at the front.

Aston Martin had been hoping that the car would be able to reach 329km/h (205mph) but, in the event, it managed 'only' 307km/h (191mph).

Unique

Just one example was built. It happily survives, having originally been acquired by an American enthusiast, although this very British Bulldog is now once again kennelled in the country of its birth.

Below: The mid-engined. left-hand-drive Bulldog in the pastoral splendour of Woburn Abbey. Note the panel on the front wing below the quarter light (there is one on either side) which conceals the door operating buttons. For night driving, a flap in the nose was lowered to reveal no less than five headlights.

Above: Open wide! The hydraulic rams used to operate the doors are usually concealed by upholstery. The fuel tank is located immediately behind the seats.

Ford Probe III 1981

The oil price rise triggered by the 1973 Arab-Israeli War and the resulting spiralling of petrol prices had a profound influence on the world's car makers. Demand for small, economical models soared and the science of aerodynamics, hitherto the preserve of sports and racing-car constructors, began to be applied by the Big Batallions to their passenger models.

One such company was Ford which, in the mid-1970s, began the manufacture of a series of concept cars that were produced under the Probe name. The first of these, Probe I, was shown at the 1979 Frankfurt Motor Show. It was a sporting two-door, three-seater coupé with roughly the same dimensions as those of the contemporary Mustang.

Hardly a Drag

Significantly, its drag coefficient was an impressive 0.25 at a time when the average American saloon was producing a figure of 0.50!

This in turn paved the way for Probe II, a four-door, family sized saloon which incorporated many of the disciplines learnt on Probe I.

In the meantime the company had been developing a new model for the European market to replace the best-selling, but ultra-conventional Cortina. It appeared in 1982 as the Sierra and was significant for incorporating new aerodynamic disciplines learnt on Probes I and II.

To prepare the public for what was a radically visual departure from previous principles, with some trepidation Ford unveiled Probe III at the 1981 Frankfurt Motor Show.

Unlike its predecessors developed in America, this was a Ford of Europe project. It attained a remarkably low Cd of 0.22, which was about twice as good as the Cortina's figure.

This wind-tunnel-refined shape incorporated aerodynamic features that are today commonplace, all of which were created so as not to

Below: A Sierra in all but name. Ford's Probe III with its aerodynamically refined lines, helped to prepare the public for a corporate shift in emphasis to wind-tunnel-tested bodywork.

obstruct air flow. The usual separate front bumper was replaced by a moulding that was an extension of the front body panel. Headlamps were flush-fitting and the window glasses were positioned as close to the bodywork as possible.

Probe III's rear profile featured a semi-fastback style related to the 'bustle' that had featured on Ford's front-wheel-drive Escort of 1980.

Space Probe

Similarly, the customary wide gaps between the wheels and arches were reduced on the Probe to prevent excessive turbulence.

The Sierra made its debut about a year later, in October 1982, and although outwardly less radical than Probe III, it gave Ford an anxious time as the public took some time to become accustomed to its radical shape.

For the record, in America, Ford responded in 1982 to Probe III with the even more

Above: Probe III's unique double rear spoiler 're-attached' the air flow to the body and helped to keep the driving wheels on the ground. Inset: Note the purpose-designed wing mirrors and closeness of the front tyres to the arch.

futuristic IV, while the radical V of 1985 had a drag coefficient less than that of a fighter aircraft!

Honda HP-X 1984

In 1987 the Japanese motor industry built nearly 7.9 million cars and in so doing overhauled America as the world's largest car-manufacturing country. But Japan was not just about volume.

At the 1984 London Motor Show its concept cars dominated the Take a Trip into Tomorrow display. There was another Japanese surprise in evidence at the Turin event three weeks later.

There it became apparent that Honda, Japan's largest motorcycle manufacturer which had only begun to make cars in 1962, had commissioned the respected Pininfarina styling house to produce a sensational mid-engined concept car. Titled the HP-X, this stood for Honda Pininfarina Experimental.

It was a theme that reflected Honda's already formidable performance pedigree. As a manufacturer of racing motorcycles, it was perhaps inevitable that it would expand into the world of motor car racing.

Formula 1

Honda's first single-seater appeared in 1964

and this Formula 1 machine was followed by a successful Formula 2 engine in 1966. The company returned to European F2 in 1980 with a car powered by a new 2 litre, four-valve, iron block V6. The Ralt-Honda won the championship in 1981, 1983 and in the final year of 1984. It was this unit that

Below: Pininfarina's HP-X was created for Honda and designed to take advantage of the roadholding benefits of 'ground effect', as used by racing cars. Below left: The car's aerodynamic wedge-shape, made possible by the use of a mid-located V6 engine.

HP-X had no doors – access was gained by lifting the roof. Extensive use was made of electronics in the futuristic left-hand-drive cockpit

The vehicle had clearly been built to aerodynamic principles and while this was apparent from viewing the body, a similar approach was applied to the unseen underside of the car. It was specially contoured to benefit from the roadholding advantages of 'ground effect' that had by then been banned from Formula 1.

This concept car was no decorative offering. It had been built as a working prototype and played a significant role in the creation of Honda's prestigious NS-X, standing for for New Sports eXperimental, performance car, work on which had, significantly, also begun in the same year of 1984.

This mid-engined two-seater coupé was visually unrelated to the HP-X. It appeared in 1990 powered by a transversely mounted, 3 litre V6 engine based on the 2.5/2.7 litre Legend unit.

Below: To gain access to the HP-X's cockpit, the transparent roof had to be raised, as there were no doors. This feature never reached production.

formed the basis of the mid-engined HP-X.

Visually Stunning

Pininfarina was given a free hand to produce a futuristic performance two-seater. The result was a visually stunning vehicle with an advanced composite body, a wedge-shaped offering with a windscreen that evolved into a transparent Perspex roof. Visitors to Turin speculated unkindly that it would have been unbearably hot in summer and wildly impractical in rain! This canopy was further activated by the brake and acted as an air brake when a specified speed was reached.

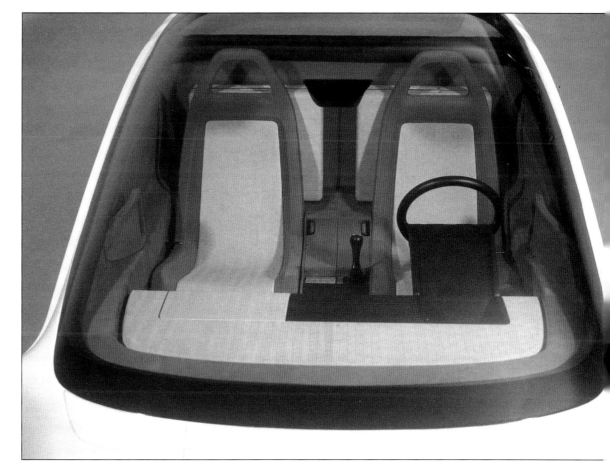

MG EX-E 1985

The last MGB sports car was built in 1980 and although the MG name survived, it did so only as an alternative badge on its parent company's saloon models.

BL Cars, custodians of the marque, made the clearest possible statement of its long-term endorsement when to, universal surprise, it unveiled a widely acclaimed mid-engined MG concept car at the 1985 Frankfurt Motor Show.

Work on the project had began at BL's Canley design studios earlier that year and the styling was the work of Gordon Sked, director of external design, under the direction of Roy Axe.

Fighter Cockpit

The MG, dubbed EX-E, was a low, finely proportioned coupé with well executed curves and a cockpit dome apparently inspired by Group C racing cars and the canopy of fighter aircraft!

Significantly the body was completely devoid of spoilers, which pointed the way forward to a new generation of cars that featured less cluttered and more aerodynamically refined lines than their predecessors.

Its structure was similar to that used for the experimental 1982 BL Technology project ECV (Energy Conservation Vehicle) 3 in that it featured an aluminium frame with external plastic panels bonded to it. The EX-E's drag coefficient was a creditable 0.24.

Although the show car was engineless, it was designed to receive the 3 litre V6 alloy engine developed for the Metro 6R4 rally car announced earlier in the year. It was also intended to be fitted with its four-wheel-drive system. Wheels were shod with substantial 7J 245/17 section tyres and top speed was a theoretical 275km/h (171mph).

The double wishbone suspension was shared with

Below: EX-E's cockpit with state-of-the-art computerized instruments. The polychromatic plastic dome was cleaned by a wiper that was automatically activated when it started to rain.

with Project XX that emerged as the Rover 800 and Honda Legend executive saloons in the following year.

The interior complemented the car's dramatic exterior. Above the red LED (light-emitting diode) display was what BL described as a 'reflex information monitor', a head-up display that featured such vital information as engine revolutions under hard acceleration and cruising speed.

There was also a futuristic telephone, the dial of which was integrated into the fascia next to a compact disc player, and a sophisticated navigation system. The microphone was attached to the headrest with sound being relayed through stereo speakers.

Well-received at Frankfurt, when an appreciative audience broke into spontaneous applause on its unveiling, the EX-E kept the MG name in the public eye, although the marque would not be truly reborn until the 1995 arrival of the much praised, mid-engined MGF. In retrospect the EX-E can be seen as representing the starting point for that project, stylistically and mechanically.

Above: EX-E's body was remarkably free of external decoration. Below: It was designed to take the potent V6 engine from the Metro 6R4 rally car.

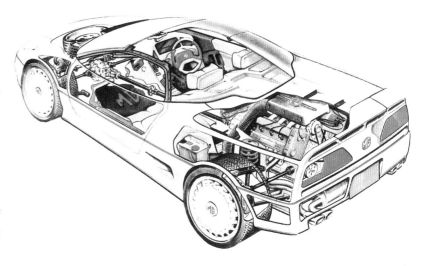

Ital Design Aztec 1988

The established Italian styling houses had to make room for a newcomer in 1968 when Giorgetto Giugiaro set up Ital Design in Italy's motoring capital of Turin. Formerly head of styling at Bertone and Ghia, he went on to essay the lines of such celebrated models as the Lotus Esprit, Volkswagen Golf and Fiats Panda and Uno.

But by 1988 Ital Design had lost its all-important Fiat commissions to the rival, and recently formed, I.DE.A concern.

At that year's Turin Show, held at Fiat's old factory in the Lingotto suburb of Turin, Giugiaro took the event by storm with no less than three related concepts: the Aspid, the Aztec and Asgard. All were mid-engined and four-wheel driven.

Asgard was a people mover, Aspid a sleek two-seater coupé with Plexiglass roof, while the related two-seater Aztec was something of a tongue-in-cheek exercise to draw the crowds. It proceeded to do just that.

Comic Strip Hero

This was because the car featured individual pods for driver and passenger who sat within transparent plastic domes in bad weather. It was an approach seemingly straight out of the pages of comic strip space hero Dan Dare.

Having said that, Ital Design maintained that this was a long-nurtured Giugiaro concept and published a 1959 sketch by the master to underline the point. One of the advantages cited for the design was good wind protection at high speeds. The detachable roof panels were small, easily removable and could be stowed under the engine cover. However, the separate wraparound windscreens were fixed in place and hinged, gull-wing style, on the cockpit dividing bar

Mapped Out

The driver's instrument panel was circular and a central console contained a futuristic computerized traffic navigation system that featured maps of

Above: The Aztec, in which each occupant had, in creator Giugiaro's words, 'room to manoeuvre'. Each individual pod was further isolated when aerodynamic domes were fitted to the top of the separate windscreens. The space age control panel is just ahead of the rear wheels.

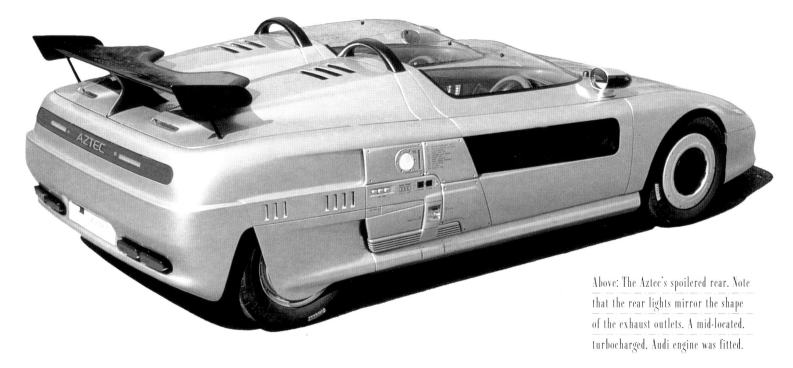

Above: The Aztec's spoilered rear. Note that the rear lights mirror the shape of the exhaust outlets. A mid-located, turbocharged, Audi engine was fitted.

city centres so that the driver could find ways of beating traffic bottlenecks. Unlike the two-pod approach, this was an idea that was destined to be translated into reality.

Below: Aztec is in the foreground, in company with its Aspid coupé and Asgard people carrier stablemates.

Power came from a mid-located, transversely mounted, turbocharged, Audi 200 2.2 litre, five-cylinder engine.

Press for Entry

The space age theme was further reinforced by the presence on each silver vehicle

of service panels positioned ahead of the rear-wheel arches. These contained three buttons and, to gain entry to the car, the driver would punch in an appropriate numerical code. This device was also used to activate the car's operating systems which included hydraulic jacks and an electric spanner to remove the wheels.

Above: The control panel followed the contours of the steering wheel. The speedometer shows 250km/h (155mph).

The Aztec remained very much a concept car, but before long Giugiaro was back with Fiat. Indeed, he was responsible for the styling of its successful and highly acclaimed Punto supermini of 1993.

Jaguar XJ220 1988

Manufacturers of one of the world's most celebrated sporting marques, the revitalized Jaguar company unveiled its XJ220 concept car at the 1988 British Motor Show. Such was the rapturous reception that greeted this silver coupé, the firm decided to put it into production.

Unlike many such vehicles, the 220 underwent a long gestation, taking nearly four years to complete. This was because it was only a semi-official project. Chairman John Egan had only agreed to the proposal of his engineering director, Jim Randle, on condition that the car was regarded as a spare-time exercise. It was consequently built by a small team of volunteers after hours and at weekends.

Big Cat Power

Randle had conceived a supercar, in the spirit of Ferrari's F40 or the Porsche 959, over the Christmas of 1984. At the 220's heart was Jaguar's mighty V12 engine but in unique 6.2 litre form. Instead of the usual single camshafts, more powerful twin overhead units would be used.

The engine was located in the mid-position and drove all four wheels courtesy of a FF Developments system. It also boasted adaptive suspension and anti-lock brakes.

Two alternative body styles were contemplated, one by Cliff Rudell and the second by Keith Helfet; the latter's version was chosen in April 1987.

Scissor Doors

The aluminium body itself was handbuilt by Park Sheet Metal of Coventry and the result was a low, sleek coupé in which the V12's mid-location was highlighted by the presence of elongated side air intakes. The scissor doors were in the Lamborghini Countach idiom.

As the 220 was conceived as a road car, the interior was well equipped with air conditioning and plush leather upholstery. The space needed to accommodate the mid-located power unit ensured that the car could only be a genuine two-seater.

Although Sir John Egan (knighted 1986) had given the project his approval, he had never seen the 220 during its development and did not do so until 10th October 1988, just eight days before the Motor Show opened its doors at Birmingham's National Exhibition Centre.

He liked what he saw and the car accordingly made its

Below left: XJ 220's sober interior. Right and below: Unlike the production car, the original 220 was V12, rather than V6, powered and accordingly longer, with scissor-type doors.

surprise appearance at the event. The public's response was such that Jaguar was encouraged to put the 220 into production.

However the company, privatized in 1984, was then taken over by Ford in November 1989. Happily, the following month it was decided to proceed with the project.

The production version did not arrive until 1992 and this turned out to be a simplified two-wheel-drive car powered by a twin turbocharged 3.5 litre V6 engine rather than a V12. A superb concept, nevertheless, its sales were overshadowed by the recession. Eventually, 275 rather than the projected 350 examples were built.

General Motors Impact 1990

Late in 1996 General Motors, the biggest of America's Big Three car makers, put the EV1, its first electric vehicle, into production. This initiative sprang from GM's Impact concept car that was unveiled in 1990.

The stimulus for the Corporation to develop this project was the California Clean Air Act which required that 10 per cent of all new cars sold in the state by 2003 should have zero exhaust emissions. The only powered vehicle that can meet this requirement is the electric car.

While such vehicles have been around for almost as long as the automobile, the Impact sports coupé did not feature the long-awaited breakthrough in battery technology that is so essential to make it a truly viable proposition.

Electric Concept

It did, however, have the virtue of having been designed from the outset as an authentic electric car rather than a modified petrol-engined one.

To offset the weight of its batteries, much of the Impact's structure was made of composite materials and the glass-fibre coupé bodywork, created by in-house Opel, recorded a drag coefficient of 0.19 – the lowest ever achieved in the GM wind tunnel.

Impact turned the scales at 998kg (2200lb) with the batteries accounting for a substantial 408kg (900lb).

There were 32 of these sealed 10-volt lead acid AC Delco units that ran centrally along the length of the car, forming a sort of 'transmission tunnel'.

At the Impact's heart was a unit that converted DC power to AC current. As a result, more efficient three-phase AC electric motors could be used. Two of them drove the car's front wheels and, accordingly, no

Below: Impact had the advantage of being designed from the outset for electric power. The body was glass-fibre.

weighty differential or gearbox were needed.

Dynamic Braking

A further innovation was the use of regenerative braking which meant that the electric motors were transformed into dynamos that charged the batteries when the driver applied the brakes.

A two-seater, the Impact was intended to be a short-distance car. GM claimed a top speed of 161km/h (100mph) and a 0 to 96km/h (60mph) acceleration figure of eight seconds. It had a range of 193km (120 miles) but the batteries needed recharging every six hours.

This requirement underlined the need for improvements in battery technology, and in 1991 General Motors joined with its Ford and Chrysler rivals to pool their research in this crucial area.

It was another six years before EV1 entered production in 1996 and, although outwardly resembling the Impact concept, some significant changes had been made below the surface. Unlike the original, which had two electric motors, the production version has one and thus fewer batteries.

While EV1 is suitable for use in towns, it must be admitted that the viable long-distance electric car is not yet a feasible proposition.

Above: There was no exhaust pipe and the car's impressive aerodynamics were aided by a smooth undertray. Its low drag coefficient, about half that of the average family saloon, was also aided by an absence of bumpers.

Below: All that could be seen of the electric power unit. The suitcase-sized box contained the converter that transformed the DC current, supplied by the batteries, to the AC power which operated the motors.

Ital Design Columbus 1992

Created by Ital Design to commemorate the 500th anniversary of the discovery of America, Columbus was intended as a luxurious and sophisticated people carrier.

Giugiaro's idea was to produce an alternative to the elongated sedan, so beloved of American executives and personalities, replacing it with a large but well-proportioned vehicle.

Ample Seating

Able to carry nine passengers, or seven if alternative seating arrangements were used, Columbus featured a carbon-fibre four-door body with opening hatchback. It was nearly 6096mm (20 feet) long.

Power came from BMW's 5 litre V12 engine, positioned transversely in the middle and on the left-hand side of the vehicle. Computer-controlled drive was taken, via a five-speed ZF gearbox, to all four steerable wheels. Ingeniously, those at the rear moved within a limited 15 degree arc.

As presented at the 1992 Turin Motor Show, Columbus was displayed in its more spacious VIP seven-seater form. The plush leather-lined interior seemed to have more in common with a Jumbo jet than a road vehicle.

The driver's seat was positioned centrally in the forward compartment with a commanding view through the forward bubble. Two people could be accommodated in two seats behind that and the remaining four individuals occupied the lower rear level.

Touring Mode

If nine occupants were carried in Columbus's tourist mode, the steering wheel was moved to the left. One person would sit alongside the driver and two

Below: Aimed at the American market, the appropriately named Columbus was intended to replace the elongated sedans so beloved by film, TV and pop stars.

behind. A further five could occupy the rear compartment, four of them sharing the comfortable double seats.

The instrument panel echoed that of BMW's prestigious 8 Series cars, although an extra two dials had been added. One showed the temperatures in the compartments – they had separate air conditioning units – the other was a display which indicated the degree to which the rear wheels had turned.

Monitoring the Road

The occupants also benefited from no less than six liquid crystal monitors, two of which were fitted into the instrument panel for use by the driver.

All were connected to two cameras, one of which was at the rear to replace the customary mirror, while the other at the front enabled the rear occupants to see the road ahead.

These proved useful because Columbus was moved under its own power to Turin, the Ital Design team having worked right through Easter to get the vehicle completed in time for the event.

Giugario also chose the '92 Turin Show as the venue to unveil his minuscule Biga city electric car. By doing so, an automotive David and Goliath shared the same stand.

Below: The roomier VIP version of Columbus with seating for seven.

Above: Access was excellent for a vehicle designed to accommodate seven or nine occupants. The centrally-positioned driving seat, and its two attendant ones, were on a higher level.

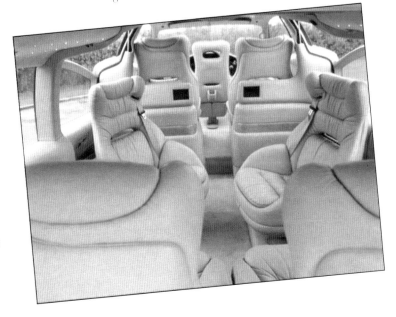

Porsche Boxster 1993

After an unhappy flirtation with front-engined grand tourers, by the early 1990s the German specialist car maker Porsche had decided to revert to its sports-car roots.

This was a tradition exemplified by its long-running and continually evolving 911. At the 1993 Detroit Motor Show the company unveiled the related Boxster, an open, two-seater, mid-engined concept car.

The venue was a wholly appropriate one because America is Porsche's largest export market. The name chosen was a combination of two elements; it referred to the boxer motor, which is what Europeans call the horizontally opposed engine used by Porsche, and the 356-based Speedster design that was created for American customers in the 1950s.

There were also mechanical and stylistic echoes of the 550 Spyder of similar vintage that was the firm's first sports racer. But the Boxster's lines also looked forward as well as back.

Silver Roadster

Outwardly it was the work of Grant Larson, a young American Porsche stylist. The silver roadster brought an appreciative response at Detroit, it looked good from its neat asymmetrical headlamps and distinctive curved doors, to the flush rear lights that incorporated LED (light-emitting diode) technology.

Adventurous Interior

The interior, the work of Stefan Stark, was equally adventurous. It included an aluminium instrument surround that played host to five dials with the revolution counter in pride of place. A novel feature was that the calibrations were engraved on the covering glass.

Below: While the 1993 Boxster concept car outwardly resembled the production version of three years later, it differed in detail: namely the curved doors and wheels that were not continued.

An LCD (liquid-crystal display) screen was positioned in the centre of the dashboard and it included a radio, TV/video, navigational aid, on-board computer system and the inevitable telephone.

The exposed gear lever on the transmission tunnel was set in an aluminium console that also contained two miniature cooling fans and ventilation controls.

Mechanical details were harder to come by at Detroit, although it was clear that this show car was intended to be mid-engined with the location of the projected power unit indicated by small air intakes just below the doors.

If the car's debut had been intended as a kite-flying exercise by a beleaguered company, it certainly succeeded because the Boxster was identified as an undoubted 'hit'. Within a month, Porsche announced that it would be putting the car into production. But it was 1996 before it was well and truly ready for the road.

Outwardly the production Boxster bears a close resemblance to the 1993 concept, although such features as the curved doors, air intakes and delicately contrived interior have succumbed to the realities of the manufacturing process. The engine is a 2.5 litre, water-cooled six, a boxer motor of course . . .

Below: The concept's dashboard: the metal finishes, exposed gear change and LCD screen have not survived. The current car has only three dials.

Plymouth Prowler 1993

Below: The steering column-mounted rev counter of the '93 concept car survives on this production model. The automatic gearbox is a four-speed Autostick unit.

Based on that peculiarly American institution, the hot rod, the Plymouth Prowler was one of the unquestioned stars of the 1993 Detroit Motor Show. Like its Dodge Viper stablemate, it is destined for production.

Conceived by the parent Chrysler Corporation's design chief, self-confessed hot-rod nut Tom Gale, in 1991, the car was not completed until mid-1992 – well in time for the Detroit Show at the beginning of the following year.

Chrome-Plated

An uncompromising open two-seater, the rear-drive Prowler was powered by a 3.5 litre, 24-valve V6 engine, complete with a hot rod's obligatory plated components, that came courtesy of Chrysler's newly introduced front-wheel-drive Concorde saloon. However, a chromed exhaust manifold helped to boost output from 214 to 240bhp.

The Concorde also furnished the Prowler with its transaxle that incorporated four-speed automatic transmission, although in this instance it was

Below: Little of the vitality of the original concept has been lost on the production Prowler. After some delays, deliveries began in 1997.

transferred from the front to the rear of the car.

Suspension was independent all round with double wishbones exposed at the front; the rear layout was also Concorde-sourced.

Despite its wacky image, the Prowler featured such conventional elements as power-assisted steering, airbags for both driver and passenger and power-operated hood. The front bumper was removable, and the headlamps stylishly followed the contours of the narrow nose.

The body of the skimpy convertible with cycle-type front

wings contributed little structural strength, so the Prowler was based on a substantial channel-section aluminium chassis.

Purple Heart

Having built one car, Chrysler's mandarins were soon contemplating the prospects for manufacturing a production version. The project was given the corporate green light in September 1994 with the Prowler intended to enter production three years later. The first 300 examples were destined to be finished in striking purple livery.

Although the production version basically resembles the show car, it differs from it in a number of important respects. The body is both longer and

wider; there is a more substantial front bumper; and the headlamps have been enlarged. A hair-raising 201km/h (125mph) top speed is envisaged.

The car is being built at Chrysler's so-called 'toy factory' which also produces the Dodge

Viper, which also began life as a concept car at the '89 Detroit show and subsequently entered production in 1992.

A very real commercial bonus is that the way-out Prowler will also help to raise the profile of Chrysler's hitherto lack-lustre Plymouth division.

Above: The Prowler loses much of its boot space when the hood is lowered. So Chrysler has produced this matching luggage trailer for touring.

Below: It's not often that a car's independent front suspension is on view. The Prowler uses double wishbones with pushrod-actuated shock absorbers.

Volkswagen Concept 1 1994/95

Volkswagen's Beetle is the best-selling car in the history of the automobile. It is still in production in Mexico where the 21 millionth example was completed in 1991.

The car has cast a long shadow over the history of a company that came into being to mass-produce it. After 50 years of continuous production, German manufacture effectively ceased in 1978. Then at the 1994 Detroit Motor Show Volkswagen revealed Concept 1, outwardly a spiritual successor of the legendary original.

Created at VW's American Design Centre, located at Simi Valley, California, the car began life in 1992 as an electrically powered vehicle. It looked the way it did to induce the public to buy it. Styling took place in the presence of a 1948 Beetle.

It was the work of J. Carroll Mays, who went on to become head of design at in-house Audi. Although the show car was powered by an electric motor from a golfing trolley, it was envisaged that conventional engines would be used in production versions.

Unlike the original 1938 design which employed a rear-located, air-cooled, flat-four engine, this was a modern front-wheel-drive car. It was based on the platform that played host to the Seat Ibiza and the following year's Golf.

The interior reflected contemporary thinking with some echoes of the original. Its single round gauge incorporated the speedometer, engine temperature gauge, fuel gauge and headlight switch.

Automatic transmission was employed, and air conditioning, twin airbags, side impact bars as well as an automatic braking system, all featured as part of the package. Like the original, it was designed to accommodate four adults.

Cabriolet Version

Following an appreciative response at Detroit, a cabriolet version of the design was displayed at the Geneva Motor Show. In November 1994, following encouraging market

WOB • 1994

Left: Concept 1, designed by VW's American studio, as it appeared at the 1994 Detroit Motor Show. Above: A cabriolet version arrived three months later at the Geneva Show. The 'screen pillars acted as a rollover bar.

research findings in America, Vollkswagen decided to put the vehicle into production before the year 2000.

With this in view, management of the project was transferred from the US to Germany and a design team under Hartmut Warkub assigned responsibility for the project.

VW displayed a further development of the concept at the 1995 Tokyo Motor Show. It

differed from the 1994 studies by being both slightly wider and longer, and having integrated bumpers and enlarged circular headlamps. A further refinement was the presence of a sunroof that looked black from the outside, but which

from the inside allowed the car's occupants to enjoy a clear view of the sky.

The intention is to produce the car in Mexico. It will share a platform with the new Golf which arrives in 1998, and be built in 1.3, 1.4 litre and also

1.9 diesel forms for the mainly American market. A right-hand-drive version will also be available for Britain.

Below: Evolution of a theme: the 1995 version was both longer and wider than the previous year's concept. Changes were also made to the rear profile to permit an increased amount of headroom.

Mercedes-Benz MCC 1994

After devoting its formidable talents to producing some of the world's largest and most expensive cars, Mercedes-Benz has performed a marketing somersault and is going small-minded. A new supermini arrives in 1997 and the minuscule Smart city car will follow in 1998.

This is a project that began in 1990 with the Swiss SMH group that also created the Swatch watch. Originally backed by Volkswagen, that company withdrew from the scheme in January 1993 but it was secretly taken up by Mercedes-Benz.

Early in 1994 it unveiled the MCC, which stands for Micro Concept Car. It was being developed in two forms; the Eco-Speedster and Eco-Sprinter, respectively powered by petrol and electric engines. Both were the same length, a mere 2500mm (98in), a figure which makes the Mini appear positively palatial at 3038mm (120in) long.

Safety Features

Great attention was paid to the occupants' protection and the MCC's substructure contained no less than 29 safety features which, unusually, included door-mounted air bags.

Both of these tiny cars incorporated Mercedes' ingenious 'sandwich' principle that was shared with the projected supermini. This sited the power unit beneath the floor. It was located at the front of the larger car, but in the two MCCs the compact engines were rear-mounted.

These three-door hatchbacks were two-seaters. Although the electric version was slightly narrower, to provide occupants with the maximum shoulder room, the passenger's seat was mounted 300mm (12in) behind the driver's.

The petrol-fuelled Speedster would use a three-cylinder turbocharged engine that drove the rear wheels. However, the electric-powered Sprinter was front-wheel driven.

California Dreaming

In their concept forms both vehicles featured aluminium extruded substructures with plastic body panels. Styling, the work of Mercedes-Benz's Californian studios, has taken rather longer than anticipated to resolve and the cars have

Opposite: Announced in 1994, the petrol-fuelled Eco-Speedster (right) was aimed at the youth market. The Eco-Sprinter used electric power.

Above: Smart's diminutive steering wheel. Initially, only left-hand-drive cars will be built. Versions for the UK market may not arrive until 2000.

passed through a number of evolutionary visual phases. There have also been some mechanical alterations and a semantic one – the Smart name was announced in May 1995 as a replacement for MCC.

The petrol version car is to be manufactured first at the rate of 200,000 units per annum, in a new £305 million factory built at Sarreguemines in north-eastern France. It is planned that production in America and Asia will follow.

Mercedes-Benz hope that these potentially high-sales-volume models will help to increase its annual production that stands at around the 500,000 mark. The rest of the industry is watching with the keenest interest to see if this corporate gamble will pay off.

Above: By 1995 the design of the Smart had changed somewhat, as this mock-up indicates. The model will be launched at the 1997 Frankfurt Motor Show.

Chrysler Atlantic 1995

Chrysler did not disappoint the crowds at the 1995 Detroit Motor Show. There it unveiled a trio of concept cars, of which the most memorable was the Atlantic coupé with its lines deeply rooted in the 1930s.

Unlike the earlier Dodge Viper and Plymouth Prowler show cars, however, there is no likelihood of this daring trip down an automotive memory lane ever reaching the production line.

Chrysler's president, Robert A. Lutz, is an old-car enthusiast and collector of long-standing. He was thus familiar with the fabulous French sports coupés of the 1930s, and the products of the legendary Bugatti company in particular.

Napkin Design

The concept for the Atlantic emerged during a 1993 conversation that Lutz had with his design chief, Tom Gale. In the best stylistic traditions, he is reputed to have sketched the design on the back of a table napkin. Gale in turn appointed a team headed by Jack Crain to turn Lutz's dream into a reality.

Once the design was completed, the project was contracted to Metalcrafters in Southern California. This is a company that has been producing Chrysler concept cars since 1979.

The Atlantic was constructed around a tubular chassis that united Dodge Viper front and rear sub-frames. The all-independent suspension and steering gear came from the same source.

Bugatti Pastiche

Nineteen-thirties Bugatti influence was readily apparent under the bonnet. Bugatti's cars had been powered by a 3.3 litre, twin-overhead-camshaft, straight-eight engine and this latter-day pastiche used an eight-cylinder, 4 litre

Below: The Atlantic: an extraordinary, but successful, blend of 1930's French and latter day American themes. Unlike other Chrysler concept cars, this one is unlikely to enter production. It even has a straight-eight engine.

Left: The instruments resembled the faces of Swiss watches and were the work of young Chrysler designer. Michael Castiglione. They also featured on the console which had a 'woven' appearance.

Below: The Atlantic's 'Bugatti inspiration' is particularly apparent at the rear which imitated the contours of the legendary French make's Atalante model. The quality and detail is particularly impressive.

twin-cam created by mounting two 16-valve fours, courtesy of the firm's Neon saloon, on a common crankcase. A stylish cambox completed the underbonnet architecture.

The steel bodywork, styled by Bob Hubbach, was a glorious synthesis of essentially Bugatti themes, which incorporated elements of the fabulous Atalante and even rarer Atlantic coupés, from which the Chrysler derived its name. Having said that, the strong curvilinear influences of 1990s' Detroit have made themselves felt. This is a big car that is enhanced by 559mm (22in) diameter wheels.

A two-plus-two seater with an interior the work of a young Chrysler designer, Michael Castiglione, the Atlantic was luxuriously upholstered in cream leather. The instrument surrounds and door cappings were not made of wood. This was considered to be too predictable. Instead they were clad in a man-made maroon coloured material with a woven carbon-fibre look to it. It provided a stylish backdrop for the instruments with dials that boasted the clarity of a classic Swiss watch. They were in fact non-working dummies, but then you can take such liberties with a concept car.

Ford GT90 1995

The favourable publicity generated by Chrysler's series of concept cars did not go unnoticed by Ford; the result was the GT90, created at the cost of $1,000,000. Announced at the 1995 Detroit Motor Show, it also gave the public its first view of what the company called its New Edge styling.

This impressively styled supercar was a spiritual successor to the mid-engined GT40 that earned Ford no fewer than four successive wins at the Le Mans 24-hour race between 1966 and 1969.

Built by the company's Special Vehicle Operations division, the car's starting point was a V12 created with the intention of displaying Ford's flexibility in modular engine construction.

The GT90 used a 90 degree 12 that derived from the V8 used in the Lincoln Mark III. It was constructed by lopping the rear two and front two cylinders off two of these engines, and then ingeniously grafting what remained together.

This produced a 5.9 litre unit, the performance of which was enhanced by the presence of no fewer than four turbochargers. Developing 720bhp, it gave the GT90 a theoretical top speed of 378km/h (235mph). It was mid-located in a honeycombed aluminium monocoque of the type used by Ford-owned Jaguar for its XJ220 supercar. This version was lengthened to accommodate a V12 rather than a V6 engine.

On the Edge

The mechanicals were cloaked in a body made of carbon-fibre panels. The GT90's distinctive appearance marked the arrival of what Ford initially called its 'edge' styling. The company's director of advanced design, Tom Scott, did not want a 'soft' shape for the GT90. Instead its lines were inspired by Group C sports racers. He let the surfaces of the car's body be dictated by the airflow that turned and rolled as the air pattern advanced. The natural intersections that resulted created an edge that was transformed into a design feature. The repetition of triangular forms also became a complementary design influence both inside and out.

Below: The carbon-fibre-bodied GT90 with lines that were inspired by Group C racers and the stealth fighter! This was the first example of what Ford calls its current New Edge styling.

Red Light District

The GT90's interior was well (but not luxuriously) appointed. The rear pillar, which is something of a blind spot on such machines, had an infra-red beam mounted in it. The driver is alerted to an approaching vehicle by a red light on the dashboard.

But why GT90? The initials reflected its famous GT40 predecessor, while 90 referred to the decade in which the car was built. Simple really.

Top: The exhaust pipes emerge from a collar made from material that NASA uses for the Space Shuttle. Triangular themes abound. Above: The front is unashamedly retro and recalls the GT40 of the 1960s.

The latter theme was particularly apparent on the massive engine air intakes and at the back of the car where four exhaust pipes emerged from a triangular-shaped cuff just 6.35mm (0.25 in) deep. It was made of a ceramic material of the type used on the Space Shuttle and capable of withstanding temperatures of 538°C (1,000°F).

Asia Motors Neo Mattina 1995

South Korea is one of the so-called tiger economies of the Far East; its increasingly robust motor industry is a mere 20 or so years old. Asia Motors, which builds military and commercial vehicles, is one of its larger elements and is now poised to enter the burgeoning four-wheel-drive market.

Asia revealed its visually stunning Neo Mattina concept at the 1995 Seoul Motor Show. This was a vehicle that would not have looked out of place in a Star Wars film and that could have been appropriate transport for Judge Dredd.

Lotus Lines

This futuristic-looking vehicle did not, however, hail from the South Korean industry, which usually adopts bland and rather unadventurous styling for its products. Mattina was designed in Britain, or more specifically the Norfolk village of Hethel that is the home of Lotus Design.

It was the work of Julian Thompson, Russell Carr and David Brisbourne who worked in close conjunction with Asia's design chief, Won Chul Cho, a former student of the Royal College of Art in London.

Neo Mattina was built on a widened and extended version of the Kia Sportage's ladder chassis. It was chosen because Kia is Asia Motors' largest shareholder and as such it also produces that company's Pride hatchback at its Kwang-Ju factory.

Cross-Country Capability

Regarded as Asia's response to the Land-Rover Discovery, the silver Mattina combined the cross-country attributes of four-wheel-drive with the carrying capacity of a multi-purpose vehicle – seven passengers could be accommodated.

It was visually dominated by a powerful seven-bar radiator grille that was combined with the minimum of frontal overhang and a distinctly forward driving position. The vehicle also had a high ground clearance that underlined its cross-country attributes.

Despite having used the Sportage chassis for the concept vehicle, Asia is also contemplating two alternatives before it puts the Neo Mattina in production. It might use the platform of Kia's new medium-sized Credos saloon that was derived from the Mazda 626. If this is not feasible, then it may design its own monocoque, which would be a far more satisfactory, but more expensive, solution.

As far as a power unit is concerned, Rover's new 2.5 litre K-Series V6 would seem to be a prime candidate as this is already used in the Credos. Other possibilities are turbocharged diesel units from Rover or the Italian VM concern.

Left: Artist's impression of the Lotus-designed, four-wheel-drive, Neo Mattina with high ground clearance for cross-country work. Asia hopes to have it in production by the 21st century. When the concept was completed, the doors were redesigned to be centre opening.

A Cool Half Million

Asia is aiming to produce 500,000 vehicles per annum by the year 2000 which is a considerable increase on the 200,000 it builds at the moment. Of this total, it is hoped that the four-wheel-drive/MPV hybrid will account for some 100,000 units. But of one thing we can be certain: Neo Mattina will be a very real head turner!

Right: Notable features of the vehicle are its short front and rear overhangs and its large area of glass. There is seating accommodation for seven people.

BMW Just 4/2 1995

computer work and crash simulation. The vehicle itself took a mere, but hectic, 12 weeks to assemble.

Before it began producing cars in 1928, BMW built motorcycles and it still does so today. It was, therefore, wholly appropriate that Just 4/2, which it exhibited at the 1995 Tokyo Motor Show, was a combination of these two concepts and with leanings towards two wheels rather than four!

This audacious rear-engined two-seater lacked the usual niceties of doors and weather protection and was clearly not for the fainted hearted. It was the work of BMW's M-Technik think tank and, in particular, 41 year old Robert Powell.

Below: Just 4/2's spaceframe used no less than 20 different types of aluminium extrusion. Although a BMW K1100 motorcycle engine was employed, the gearbox was a car unit which provided a reverse gear. The all-independent suspension was exposed to view and, accordingly, polished. Lights, wings and bumpers were all street legal.

Just for Who?

Just 4/2 was built as the result of an internal corporate competition and it particularly impressed BMW's technical director, Wolfgang Reitzle. Today he is chairman of the company's Rover subsidiary which originally sponsored Powell at the Royal College of Art.

Powell's inspiration was a no-frills car like the Caterham Seven. The project took about a year to complete, approval having been given in the autumn of 1994. It went through the obligatory development process under the watchful eye of Technik's supremo, Mario Theissen, and involved 100 engineers throughout the company.

The design process was similar to that applied to BMW's mainstream models, so a clay model was initially produced and there followed

Aluminium Spaceframe

Just 4/2 was built up around an aluminium spaceframe chassis. The power unit, courtesy of BMW's K1100 motorcycle, was a 1.1 litre, 16-valve, four-cylinder unit that was mounted transversely at the rear. If the car's occupants were unwise enough to bring any belongings with them, these could be stored in a bin mounted on top of the engine.

All-independent strut suspension was employed front and rear while the disc brakes were courtesy of BMW's

Right: Is it a car or a motorcycle? Although this was a futuristic concept, there could be little doubt that Just 4/2 was a BMW. The radiator and battery were crammed into the nose. Top speed was in excess of 177km/h (110mph) and acceleration shattering.

Below: The instrument panel was, inevitably, basic. The knurled wheels in the foreground were for adjusting the position of the lightweight carbon-fibre seats. The seats were lined with a thin layer of foam and incorporated tilting backs.

prestigious M3 model. Their presence was all too apparent because of the adoption of wide-spaced, handsome three-spoked alloy wheels.

Body panels, such as they were, were removable and made of Kevlar which is a carbon-fibre material. This was also used for the seat backs. The squabs incorporated a novel form of fore and aft adjustment.

Lightweight

With essentials pared to the absolute minimum, Just 4/2 turned the scales at a mere 550kg (1212lb). This helped it to reach 100km/h (62mph) in just six seconds.

BMW was sufficiently encouraged by its reception at

Tokyo to begin a test programme. This does not necessarily mean that a Just 4/2 production model is likely, but the company was

sufficiently interested in the concept to start work on a second version that was completed at the end of 1995.

Audi TT 1995

The Audi TT is very much more than an unashamed piece of 1930s' nostalgia. Unveiled at the 1995 Frankfurt Motor Show, it assuredly incorporated over 60 years of German stylistic themes, yet remained wholly modern in conception.

The TT began life at the Volkswagen Audi Design Centre in California, the same facility that was responsible for VW's Beetle-inspired Concept 1.

There, in May 1994, German/American stylist, Freeman Thomas, began work on a series of sketches that drew swift and positive approval from his boss, J. Mays, head of Audi design.

He in turn enlisted the support of the A4 project manager, Dr Ulrich Hackenburg, and corporate R and D chief, Josef Paefgen. Work soon began in Germany on what the world now knows as the TTS roadster that was to be exhibited at the 1995 Frankfurt motor show.

Coupé Coup

But some two months into the project, VW Audi's chairman, Ferdinand Piech, had a change of heart. He decided that because other manufacturers were working on open concept cars to display at the event, his company would opt instead for a coupé version.

Unlike similar vehicles, the TT was a particularly cost-conscious project and drew on components and expertise generated from existing models in the Audi range, as well as those under development.

Below: The acclaimed four-wheel-drive TT concept. which incorporated old and new Germanic themes. is scheduled to enter production in 1997.

It was based on a shortened platform for the projected front-wheel-drive A3 hatchback of 1996. This important building block was to be shared with the new VW Golf and featured a transversely located engine, rather than Audi's customary in-line unit.

However, the TT used a 150bhp 1.8 litre four, courtesy of the Audi A4 range. The company's pioneering, and leech-like, Quattro four-wheel-drive system was employed.

The body incorporated aluminium doors, bonnet and boot lid and used technology developed for the acclaimed top-line A8 saloon.

Above: Unlike the coupé which can carry children in the back, the open version is a two-seater. Right: The instrument panel is very simple, with aluminium and leather used to effect.

Nostalgia

Nostalgic elements were also incorporated in the six-spoked wheels that echoed those used on Bugatti racing and sports cars of the inter-war years.

Romanian designer Romulus Rost was responsible for the interior and, like the exterior, the emphasis was on clean and simple themes that were highlighted by the use of aluminium and leather. This was a two-plus-two seater with folding seats to permit access for children in the rear.

Completed in seven hectic months, the coupé was greeted with much acclaim at its Frankfurt debut, after which Audi announced that it would be putting the TT into production. This was underlined when the roadster was subsequently unveiled at the Tokyo show. The model is destined to appear in front-wheel-drive form at the end of 1997, although Quattro versions may also be offered.

Vauxhall Maxx 1995

Maxx, unveiled at the 1995 Geneva Motor Show, was produced in response to a survey of European motorists which revealed that half of them wanted a personalized car. It would allow customers to be able to choose between city car bodywork or the pick-up, convertible or off-road options.

Designed at General Motors-owned Vauxhall's Technical Development Centre at Russelsheim, Germany, at Maxx's metallic heart was a spaceframe of aluminium extrusions. Its overall length of 2975mm (9ft 7in) meant that it was some 750mm (29in) shorter than the Corsa which is Vauxhall's smallest current production car.

Plastic Maxx

The aluminium frame broke surface on the body at the waistband, which incorporated a reinforcing crash belt. The remainder of the body was made of clip-on plastic or composite panels.

Power was courtesy of GM's new three-cylinder, cast-iron, Ecotech lean-burn engine. A twin-overhead-camshaft, 12-valve unit of 973cc, it replaced the Corsa's existing 1.2 litre four in 1997. Frontally and transversely mounted, it drove the front wheels via a five-speed electrically actuated sequential gearbox.

This meant that upward and downward gearchanges could be achieved by the use of a rocker switch conveniently located by the steering wheel. However, if the driver found this too arduous, another control converted the 'box to automatic transmission.

Suspension was essentially conventional with front MacPherson struts, and torsion beam suspension at the rear. This was used in conjunction with forward-inclined struts to permit the maximum of luggage to be stowed in the vehicle's rear compartment.

Below: Although not apparent. Maxx is front-engined. with three cylinders.

Swivel Seat

The interior of this concept car featured a swivelling bench-type front seat that could be moved with the driver and passenger in situ. This allowed access to the rear seats, that folded, and the luggage compartment.

Ahead of the driver was a wide padded dashboard based on an extruded aluminium crossmember. This all-important C-beam was at the heart of Maxx's modular design.

Further scope for customer choice was possible with regards to interior fittings. For instance analogue or digital displays and accessories such

as passenger airbag and air conditioning could be specified. These could even be retrospectively fitted as another simple module, along with various audio options and even a built-in telephone, navigation or fax system.

The firewall that separated the car's occupants from the engine incorporated a strong, rupture-proof corrugated aluminium sandwich.

General Motors produced two driveable versions of Maxx. Engine apart, it will be interesting to see what elements of its revolutionary specifications reach the production line.

Above: General Motors displayed a longer wheelbase, four-door version, badged as an in-house Opel, at the 1995 Geneva Motor Show. A roadster version was also contemplated but has not yet been built.

Below: Cockpit of the two-door version. The front seat swivels on a central pivot to permit access to the luggage space behind. Note the fascia which is mounted on an extruded aluminium cross-member.

Honda SSM 1995

Acclaimed as the star of the 1995 Tokyo Motor Show, the SSM, which stands for Sports Study Model, may enter production in an attempt by Honda to sharpen its sporting image, particularly on the important European market.

Unlike the company's acclaimed mid-engined NSX, the SSM featured more traditional mechanicals and, as such, was a traditional front-engine/rear-drive concept.

Honda's first sports car was the feisty S800 coupé of 1966-70 vintage and the SSM reverted to its engine and drive configuration, although it was an open two-seater.

Innovation and Tradition

Created in-house at the Wako Design Centre near Tokyo, Honda maintained that it showed 'the company at its innovative best applying state of art solutions to a traditional sports car concept.'

With well proportioned, uncluttered lines, the SSM featured a steel monocoque shell with wraparound twin cockpits. Each was lined with composite panels and had its own rollover hoop. They were divided by a robust reinforcing bar which made a significant contribution to the stiffness of the body structure.

The driver enjoyed a state-of-the-art instrument package with a liquid-crystal display pack, air conditioning and computerized navigation system. A distinctive red button on the right of the cockpit was used to start the engine.

This was a 2 litre, five-cylinder, twin-overhead-camshaft, VTEC 20-valve unit. The NSX-derived F-Matic transmission had five speeds and finger-tip control. Suspension also came courtesy of the prestigious sports car and employed machined aluminium wishbones all round.

Below: Refreshingly conventional, the front-engine/rear-drive SSM which may enter production in 1998. A 2 litre, five-cylinder engine was fitted. Pictured at the 1996 British International Motor Show held at Birmingham's NEC.

Above: The SSM's neat rear view. It is right-hand drive; the Japanese, like the British, still drive on the left side of the road.

Below: It seems likely that the cockpit-strengthening strut will not reach production as it somewhat restricts the occupants' shoulder space.

Enthusiastic Reception

The SSM, with a claimed top speed of 249km/h (155mph), received an enthusiastic reception from commentators at Tokyo. Honda says that it may go into production sometime in 1998.

The NSX is currently manufactured at a purpose-built factory at Tochigi designed to produce 50 cars a day and 12,000 cars per annum. It is currently operating at only some 1200 a year. The projected SSM could be a candidate for the plant. The car would probably be built using aluminium bodywork, although the rather cramped cockpit would also require more radical revision.

While Honda will persevere with its NSX flagship, it will be restyled and V12-powered. The SSM, by contrast, would only be built if it could make a profit. Honda estimates that this would have to be at the annual rate of some 20,000 units. 1998 is the favoured date as Honda's 50th anniversary falls in that year, which may also see its return to Formula 1 . . .

Mitsubishi Gaus 1995

If the Gaus name sounds unfamiliar, it is because it is an acronym for Global Adventure Utility System. It was created by Mitsubishi as a futuristic vision of a space age utility vehicle capable of on- and off-road performance.

Revealed at the 1995 Frankfurt Motor Show, a distinctive feature of the Gaus was that it was designed with three types of door. There was a conventional one on the driver's side, but its opposite number for the passengers was of the gull-wing type and there was further assymetrical one at the vehicle's rear.

The dominant but compact gull-wing unit was designed in response to Japan's busy and crowded roads. Split into two horizontal sections, the motor-driven door opened and closed at the touch of a switch. It was also fitted with its own sliding window. The top section, actuated by hydraulic arms, slid into the roof cavity, while the lower half folded down into a retractable step.

Top Glass

Gaus's upper body mostly consisted of specially treated glass that reflected away heat and filtered out ultraviolet light. This meant that the cabin temperature remained comfortable, even in the strongest sunlight.

The Gaus's long wheelbase and cab-forward design ensured that the vehicle had a spacious interior. The simple but functional instrument panel featured a dashboard-mounted gear lever. This feature, combined with the wide interior and flat floor, ensured walk-through space between the front and rear seats.

Satellite Navigation

Gaus was also equipped to take advantage of a satellite-based navigation system. Information such as road, weather and traffic conditions was displayed in the centre of the instrument panel. There it

Below: The top half of this motor-driven door opens at the touch of a switch, while the lower half forms a step.

could clearly be seen, not only by the driver, but also the passengers behind.

These occupied four separate seats. For relaxation, the front ones could be rotated to face rearwards. Conveniently, the rear seats could be folded away when Gaus was used for transporting cargo.

Power came from a front-mounted, 2 litre, turbocharged, twin-overhead-camshaft, four-cylinder engine. Transmission, a refined version of that used on the Mitsubishi Carisma, was equipped with a neural network computer. This logged each driver's different style and its gear shifting was accordingly programmed to his or her particular requirements.

Above: Gaus's instrument panel with a dashboard-mounted automatic gear lever. Left: For recreational purposes, the two front seats can be rotated to face the rear ones, which can also be folded to increase carrying capacity.

Four-wheel-drive was employed for road and cross-country use and ground clearance was enhanced by use of 457mm (18in) wheels. The wheel arches and bumper surrounds were made of a recycled plastic material.

Some elements of Gaus's radical appearance are likely to appear in Mitsubishi's next-generation Space Runner and Space Wagon multi-purpose vehicles that are due for replacement in 1998.

Ford Synergy 2010 1996

As the 20th century draws to a close, the world's car makers are actively looking for alternative power sources. Of these, electricity which boasts zero emissions is by far the preferred choice, but vehicles so powered currently only have a limited range.

To overcome this drawback, manufacturers are creating hybrids, which are powered by electricity but have their batteries charged by conventionally fuelled engines. Ford's Synergy 2010, that appeared at the 1996 Detroit Motor Show, is one of this new breed of vehicles.

It is Ford's contribution to a programme, in which it has joined forces with General Motors and Chrysler, to produce a car that can average 3.5 litres/per 100km (80mpg) by the year 2004.

Fuel Efficiency

This daringly styled six-seater coupé has something like three times the fuel efficiency of a comparable 1996 car. Weighing a mere 1000kg (2205lb), it has a drag coefficient of just 0.20.

An aerodynamically adventurous concept, designed by Ford's Rick Wells, it was found to be 40 per cent more efficient than a current Ford, thanks to the distinctive aluminium monocoque body. This featured distinctive fin-shaped front quarter panels.

They started as 305mm (12in) high, 13mm (0.5 in) wide manifolds that swept back towards the Synergy's streamlined body. Their role was to provide ventilation for the cooling system. In addition they housed cameras that replaced the usual mirrors. Furthermore they also functioned as aerodynamic devices to control the flow of air along the car's side, just as happens in a Formula 1 racing car.

Back to the Future

The rear-mounted, 1 litre, direct-injection turbo diesel engine could either be self contained, or used to generate electricity that drove a motor attached to each wheel. Interestingly, this approach is as old as the motor industry itself, and was used by Ferdinand Porsche back in far distant 1900.

In the nose of the vehicle was a flywheel which stored

Above: Synergy was a diesel/electric hybrid and featured a lightweight aluminium body. The curious and apparently unrelated front wings formed part of the car's air-extractor cooling system. They also housed rear-view cameras.

Below: The car's nose contained a flywheel that stored excess engine and braking energy. When quick acceleration was required, it could be released to augment engine power and so save fuel. Tiny, but powerful, head lamps can be seen on the forward edge of the frontal lip.

excess engine and braking energy, which was then released when the driver accelerated rapidly.

The interior was equally futuristic with most electronic controls being voice actuated.

The instrument panel consisted of a head-up display mounted on the steering column.

Synergy was designed for use on both sides of the Atlantic because an aircraft-style cantilever arm positioned in the centre of the dashboard enabled it to be swiftly converted from left- to right-hand drive. It was an appropriate feature for a vehicle created in recognition of a global climatic problem.

Below: Synergy featured pillarless construction and the roomy interior was designed to carry six people. It could also be easily converted from left- to right-hand drive by the use of an aircraft-style cantilever arm located in the centre of the dashboard.

Dodge Intrepid ESX 1996

The ESX concept car that Chrysler unveiled at the 1996 Detroit Motor Show revealed two distinct trends. In the first instance it gave some indication of the direction that Chrysler's LH-Series saloons will take when they are unveiled in 1998.

Secondly it incorporated elements of the Corporation's contribution to the American government's 2004 programme to produce an extremely fuel-efficient vehicle by that date. The production Intrepid will be conventionally powered, although the ESX diesel/ electric hybrid shared some mechanical similarities, although not stylistic ones, with Ford's Synergy 2010 concept.

Sportier Profile

The ESX aluminium four-door saloon exhibited low body lines and narrow elongated windows. The distinctive cabin-forward layout reflected the sportier profile of the Dodge marque. It was made possible by the fact that, like the Synergy, the car had a rear-mounted engine although the radiator and oil cooler were positioned at the front of the vehicle.

In the case of the ENX the engine was a diminutive 1.8 litre, three-cylinder, turbocharged diesel. This was not connected by any mechanical means to the wheels, but was rather coupled to a Kohler electrical alternator. It provided power to the batteries that drove a pair of rear mounted 100bhp electric motors from British-based company Zytek.

Bolder Batteries

The batteries were located at the front of the car and were lead acid units produced by Bolder Technologies. They were conventional units apart from the fact that, instead of incorporating plates, a film of lead was wound in a spiral in order to increase its surface area and, as a result, its density of power.

Originally created for use in cordless electric drills, no less than 150 of them were coupled together to create a 82kg (180lb) power pack that could produce 90kw. Their limitation was that, while they delivered a high level of power over a short duration, they were unable to produce energy over a long period of time.

As this was a concept car, the controls were not quite what they appeared. The mushroom gear selector was in fact a dummy and the important control switch was actually disguised as a windscreen

Left: The sleek Intrepid, a diesel/electric hybrid, was powered by a small rear-mounted, 1.8 litre, three-cylinder, turbo-charged unit that drove an alternator supplying power either to the front-mounted batteries or to the electric motors that drove the rear wheels.

wiper stalk. It turned one way for drive and the other for reverse. Otherwise the interior adopted a conventional although sporty design approach.

The accelerator pedal was positioned in the usual place. Like all electrically powered cars, the ESX performed quietly on the road and moved effortlessly to 80km/h (50mph)

which was its prescribed and respectable top speed.

Both the EHX and its conventionally powered longer wheelbase Chrysler LHX stablemate were centre stage attractions at their Detroit launch. Until the problem of restricted battery life is resolved, the hybrid electric car appears to point the way forward.

Above: The aerodynamically-honed Intrepid is Chrysler's contribution to a US government initiative that will require family cars to average a fuel consumption of 80mpg by 2004.

Below: The conventionally-powered, front-wheel-drive Chrysler LHX, also unveiled at Detroit '96, is a daring visual pointer to the next generation of the Corporation's large saloons.

Lincoln Sentinel 1996

Created by corporate parent Ford as a car that, 50 years hence, would be instantly identifiable as a Lincoln, the luxurious Sentinel made its appearance at the 1996 Detroit Motor Show.

The Lincoln marque, named after America's famous president, Abraham Lincoln, has been part of the Ford family since 1922. At that time the make was its response to General Motors' Cadillac; over the years the latter has been more successful.

To create the Sentinel, Ford director of advanced design, Claude Lobo, gathered a team of designers from the company's centres at Dearborn, USA, Dunton in Britain, Cologne, Germany and its Turin-based Ghia styling house. Once in America they visited a Classic Lincoln Club meeting.

There they not only found inspiration from Lincoln's well-regarded 1961 Continental but also from the Franco-American Facel Vega Excellence of 1958-64 vintage. Notwithstanding these influences, stylistically the finished product would have to be an utterly individual vehicle that could not be mistaken for any other.

Flagship of the Lincoln's current range is its Town Car luxury limousine. The Sentinel's wheelbase was some 560mm (22in) greater than the limousine's, even though overall the finished product was 25mm (1in) shorter.

Below: Utterly individual: the Sentinel represented a synthesis of old and new themes that included the 1961 Continental and Facel Vega Excellence.

Above: The Sentinel was powered by the 6 litre V12 engine also used in Ford's Indigo . Although the company spoke of producing a limited number. if demand exceeded 250 units annually. it seems unlikely that this Lincoln will develop beyond the concept stage.

New Edge Design

The proportions of the massive four-door glass-fibre saloon had much in common with the Excellence, as did its razor edge lines which also chimed with Ford's 'New Edge' styling that had already appeared on its GT 90 concept car. While the Sentinel also inherited elements from the big Facel Vega in the form of distinctive twin vertical headlamps and radiator grilles, the front wing line was clearly related to the '61 Continental.

Lincolns had been V12-powered since 1932 and this tradition was maintained on the Sentinel which was fitted with a new 6 litre unit. The engine also appeared in the high performance Indigo concept vehicle that shared the same stand at Detroit '96. However, Sentinel could also accommodate a supercharged V6 or a V8 with equal ease.

Stylish Ghia

The interior was not fully completed in time for the car's debut but, later in the year, Ghia fitted the Sentinel out with a New Edge interior. The idea was to show that the theme could be applied with equal success to a vehicle's dashboard and trim. Ghia was also responsible for modestly scaling down the body's proportions and highlighting the twin chromium-plated grilles on the front of the car.

While it is highly unlikely that the Sentinel could be produced in its concept car form, some commentators believe that it does point the way to the styling cues that could appear in the 1998 season. We shall just have to wait and see.

Renault Next 1996

A car with a fuel consumption of two litres of petrol per 100 kilometres, which is the equivalent of 140 miles per gallon, may sound an impossible objective, but Renault could have such a vehicle in production in 15 years time. With this aim in view, it has created the Next concept car to explore and evaluate the necessary technology.

Its aerodynamically refined, four-door, five-seater hatchback body was made of carbon-fibre and built up around an aluminium spaceframe. As a result it turned the scales at 1074kg (2368lb) which is some 90kg (198lb) less than a Renault 19. Nickel cadmium batteries accounted for a substantial 150kg (331lb) of this figure because Next is a petrol/electric hybrid.

Power was provided by a front-mounted, 750cc, three-cylinder engine. In choosing a petrol-fuelled power unit, Renault had opted for a different approach from the turbocharged diesel favoured by other manufacturers. The French company believed that harmful diesel emissions presented an obstacle which may not be satisfactorily resolved in the future.

Powerfully Charged

A five-speed manual gearbox was employed which drove the front wheels. These contained generators that, on deceleration, charged the batteries that powered 21bhp electric motors that drove each rear wheel.

At the heart of the two drive systems was an innovative computer that was able to decide whether petrol, electricity or a combination of the two should be employed.

For optimum performance the system could constantly switch from one combination to the other to the benefit of fuel consumption. As a result Next returned a figure of 3.4 litres per 100km which is a miserly, but impressive, 83mpg.

Emissions-free electric power made this particular option ideal for city driving, but

Below: Outwardly conventional yet bristling with sophistication, Next is a lightweight petrol/electric hybrid with aluminium spaceframe and plastic body panels.

the car's 167km/h (104mph) top speed was achieved with both power sources in use.

Cunning CAD

Renault produced Next, from initial sketches to rolling vehicle, in just a year by taking full advantage of computer-assisted design technology. This enabled the time-consuming prototype stage to be entirely by-passed.

Right: Next is driven by electric motors, with one powering each rear wheel, and a 48hp three-cylinder engine.

Below: Aerodynamic refinement is readily apparent in Next's appearance. The body is unpainted to help keep weight down!

The main obstacle to the company putting a Next-derived car into immediate production was its light but complex aluminium spaceframe which, at present, does not lend itself to quantity manufacture.

But Renault says that such a car could be a reality in five years time and is keeping its options open. As France's leading motor manufacturer, it knows how to produce the car, but has yet to decide whether there is sufficient popular demand for such a vehicle.

More hybrid concepts, namely Hymne, Vert and Fever, are promised and it will be extremely interesting to see what comes . . . Next.

Renault Fiftie 1996

Nineteen ninety-six marked the 50th anniversary of Renault's introduction, at the 1946 Paris Motor Show, of its rear-engined 4CV saloon.

Destined to survive until 1961, by which time over one million had been built, this milestone car was commemorated by the appearance at the Geneva Show of a concept car conceived very much in the spirit of the original.

Below: Inspired by Renault's top selling 4CV, the costly carbon-fibre bodied Fiftie was mid- rather than rear-engined.

Echoes of the Past

Created under the direction of Patrick le Quement, Renault's vice president of corporate design, the Fiftie revealed clear echoes of the 4CV enhanced by the use of modern materials. This particularly applied to the chassis that was based on Renault's innovative Sport Spider extruded-aluminium frame. The power unit was thus mid- rather than rear-located. It was Renault's new 1.1 litre, single-overhead-camshaft four that appeared simultaneously in the company's top-selling Clio supermini.

This was mated to a clutchless five-speed manual Easy gearbox that perpetuated the Ferlec control of the original. The 432mm (17in) Speedline wheels, shod with unique Michelin tyres, were also in the 4CV spirit.

There were also strong echoes at the front of the Fiftie, particularly in terms of its distinctive barred mouldings and bulbous bonnet. But unlike the original's steel structure, the body panels were made of light and strong (but costly) carbon-fibre.

The lights were fanciful in their execution, with 'apostrophe' shaped lenses at the front, while the appearance of the three-piece rear units was likened by Renault to 'kites floating in the wind'.

Niftie Fiftie

Perhaps the most radical element of the Fiftie's design was the use of a Targa-style roof. Unlike the definitive

Porsche version, in which one roof panel slid below the other, on this Renault concept car the four removable roof panels were stored beneath the rear window that, in turn, folded flat.

Inside, the Fiftie perpetuated the utilitarian spirit of its famous forebear: the floor and scuttle were covered in linoleum. The lack of an obtrusive transmission tunnel was an undoubted plus. The emphasis

Right: An artist's impression of the Fiftie with the original 4CV, a four door car, mirrored underneath.

on simplicity was underlined by the use of two pedal controls that, along with the steering wheel, were adjustable because the seats were fixed.

The doors contained pockets and were lined with woven rattan, which is a high quality wickerwork. It made a pleasing visual contrast with parts of the aluminium chassis that were exposed to view. The theme was underlined by a period accessory in the form of a woven picnic basket.

Although the original 4CV enjoyed a 15-year life, Renault has no plans to put this latter-day version into production. That pricey carbon-fibre body was part of the reason why the Fiftie is reputed to have cost a cool £3 million!

Left: The Fiftie's interior. The dashboard and pedals are movable although the seats are fixed.

Ital Formula 4 1996

Below: Variations on a theme by Ital Design: the Fiat Bravo base unit (centre) flanked by bodies for the Formula Hammer (left) and the Formula 4. Both are doorless.

Variety was the keynote of Formula 4, a concept car that Ital Design revealed at the 1996 Geneva Motor Show. Revealing stylistic echoes of his Aztec of 1988, Ital's Giorgetto Giugiaro looked upon it as his version of a Harley-Davidson motorcycle. It could thus be tailored and customized to meet its owner's specific requirements which, in the case of the Formula 4, were numerous.

All Ital needed was a like-minded manufacturer to adopt the idea. The Geneva concept car was based on the front-wheel-drive floorpan of the Fiat Bravo and powered by its 2 litre, five-cylinder engine.

Cockpit Culture

It was a concept aimed specifically at young people and was intended to conjure up the spirit of a Formula 1 racing car. But rather than just carrying one person, no less than four could be accommodated. Each of the cockpits was fitted with a robust anti-roll bar, a sports-type seat belt and even its own airbag.

An open but doorless body made of a plastic material was chosen, but it could be mass-produced in steel or aluminium if necessary, while a racing version constructed in light but costly carbon-fibre was another proposed variation.

This was clearly a warm weather car because there was no hood, only aero screens for the driver and his nearest passenger.

This was just one of a number of variations available. There were numerous alternatives that included, three-, two- or even single-seater bodywork. But this was only the start of the options. Further refinements included

Right: As might be expected from its name, Formula 4 combines the concept of a racing car with accommodation for four people. Each pod has a cover which is fitted when unoccupied.

aerodynamic skirts, fins, anti-roll bars, a mini-windscreen for each occupant and even duplicated instruments for the front passenger.

Formula Hammer

Two further variations were unveiled at the Turin Motor Show two months later. Curiously called Formula Hammer, the first retained the Bravo-based platform but had more in common with a beach buggy and offered better weather protection than Formula 4.

It had a different profile and a rather less sporting front, but came complete with a windscreen that was matched

in height by a rear rollover bar. Access presented no problem because Hammer had no body sides. But it did have a hood. This could be used in conjunction with, or without, doors finished in a matching fabric material.

The most sophisticated version was the Legram in which the Bravo platform was used as the base for an elegant streamlined coupé with an impressive Cd of 0.25.

Considerable attention had been applied to the vehicle's

Above: Fun Formula. Hammer: the windscreen does duty as rollover bar.

undertray. 'Topsides much of the roof was made of a transparent material. In all, there was something to suit every taste and pocket.

Right: The ultimate version is the Legrame, an aerodynamically-honed coupé with novel transparent roof.

Bertone Slalom 1996

Right: The Opel Calibra-based Slalom with audacious headlight treatment which is echoed in the tailgate. The extended roof line means that rear space is much better than the original.

The vivid orange hue of Bertone's concept car, launched at the 1996 Geneva Motor Show, is said to have been inspired by the colour on the label of a bottle of Veuve Clicquot, which is Nuccio Bertone's favourite champagne.

Based on the platform and running gear of Opel's turbo-charged four-wheel-drive Calibra coupé, Bertone ingeniously combined the structures of a sports model with an estate car; it thus incorporated a tailgate. It was both longer and wider than the original.

The Slalom was so called because of the many intersecting and interweaving lines that featured in the design. As a result triangles and polygons abounded. In profile the car's wedge shape was reminiscent of many cars of the 1970s and endowed it with a fashionable Retro look.

Transparent Triangles

The most dramatic feature of the design were the transparent triangular sections that adjoined the bonnet sides, behind which

Above: How a Bertone stylist envisaged the Slalom with distinctive frontal treatment and batteries of headlights positioned to cater for twisting roads.

Below: Triangular themes abound on the Slalom and these are particularly apparent on the rear lights that are fashionably high-mounted.

a battery of headlamps lurked. The idea was that they could be used to illuminate twisting mountain roads because they turned with the steering in the manner of Citroën's fabled shark-nosed DS.

The three-sided theme was reinforced by the shape of the high-placed rear lamps. Even the quarter lights were triangular. The design of the adjoining tailgate was equally unconventional, incorporating a tongue of glass, hinged at its inner edge, and let into the roof.

When luggage needed to be carried, the one-piece rear seats could be folded forward against the front ones to increase the Slalom's carrying capacity which rivalled that of a small estate car. This effectively transformed it into a rapid two-seater.

For this concept car was a runner. The potent turbocharged, 2 litre, 16-valve, twin-overhead-camshaft, four cylinder engine endowed it with a top speed in excess of 225km/h (140mph), with acceleration aided by the adoption of a six-speed gearbox. This was slightly slower than the Calibra's 241km/h (150mph) on account of the car's greater weight.

Left: The tailgate extends deeply into the roof to ensure that access is excellent for the enlarged luggage area.

Orange Verve

Inside Bertone had dispensed with the General Motors instrument panel and, while retaining the dials, replaced it with a more stylish version which sat further forward than the original.

New seats and door panels were upholstered in light and dark grey and orange leather that echoed the exterior. The orange colour was also picked up in the steering wheel, indicator stalk and even the gear lever knob.

Bertone thinks that sports estates of this type will attract a growing number of buyers, although it has no plans to produce it. Maybe General Motors will take up the idea.

Ford Saetta 1996

The Saetta, announced at the Turin Motor Show in 1996, can be seen as a visual stepping stone between the GT90 concept car and Ford's quirky Ka announced six months after the Italian event.

Created by the company's Turin-based Ghia studio, the convertible was based on the as yet unannounced Ka two-door hatchback but with the roof removed and a new tail added. This was decorated with twin red painted arrows, a punning reference to the car's name. Saetta is the Italian word for arrow.

It was the work of a team headed by American Camillo Pardo and coded BE 146 Barchetta, a prefix in corporate language that indicates its Ka origins.

Secret Model

Saetta's striking appearance was chosen to disguise the lines of the still secret model, but it also had to provide the public with enough visual clues to soften the impact of Ka's unusual profile when it was finally revealed.

The production model is Fiesta-based so this two-seater concept car used the same platform. It was finished in a striking metallic blue with the angular cladding of Ford's New Edge styling highlighted in silver and grey.

The Saetta's front was more or less undiluted Ka and featured the now familiar three cornered headlamps. A letter-box-style air intake was also a distinctive feature.

There was no hood, although a central roof rib did double duty as an anti-roll bar as well as playing a reinforcing role.

The power unit, like Ka's, was Ford's trusty 1.3 litre pushrod four used in the Fiesta Classic and it accordingly drove the front wheels.

Patent Leather

Inside the Saetta reinforced the New Edge theme and external livery with seats and door panels finished in blue and silver patent leather. The dashboard of this left-hand-drive vehicle, also Ka based,

Below: The Saetta was Ford's Ka in everything but name, even if there is no open version! The central rib provides structural reinforcement.

echoed the triangular form that is now so closely identified with the style and which was picked up on the wheel knave plates.

Ford has been tightlipped about whether the public can expect to see a convertible version of Ka. But after the Turin Show, Saetta was flown to Detroit for evaluation by corporate bosses. This may herald the appearance of a soft-top version of the Fiesta coupé which is expected to be launched in 1997.

When Ka was unveiled at the Paris Motor Show in October,

it became apparent how closely the Saetta had anticipated its idiosyncratic curvilinear contours. The Ka, built in a single 1.3 litre capacity, is being manufactured by Ford's factory at Valencia, Spain.

Motoring journalists seem to be Ka enthusiasts, and it accordingly received *Autocar* magazine's Car of the Year accolade. It remains to be seen how the public will respond to a model that must represent Ford's biggest gamble since it launched the aerodynamically honed Sierra in 1982.

Top: With only two seats the rear departs somewhat from Ka but there is speculation that it will resemble a proposed open Fiesta.

Above: The colour scheme of the patent leather interior reflects that of the body with some triangular tweaks and a Fiesta instrument panel.

IDEA Vuscia 1996

The compact multi-purpose vehicle, exemplified by Renault's acclaimed Megane Scenic, is now a reality and it is just a matter of time before other manufacturers follow suit.

They will not lack for inspiration from the Italian styling houses, one of which, I.DE.A. revealed its contribution in the shape of the Vuscia at the 1996 Turin Motor Show.

What's the IDEA?

An acronym for the Institute of Development in Automotive Engineering, it is a recent recruit to their ranks, having been founded in 1978 by Franco Mantegazza, formerly of Volkswagen and Fiat-France.

Based in a restored 18th century hunting lodge at Moncalieri on the hills outside Turin, I.DE.A came to international prominence when it essayed the lines of Fiat's celebrated Tipo of 1988. The Vuscia was based on the floorpan of its acclaimed Brava four-door successor.

It was, says the company, 'intended to be a niche car produced at a limited investment and for this reason we have conserved a large percentage of Brava components, as well as the build sequence . . . while creating a truly original shape.'

The Brava's wheelbase was extended by 200mm (7.9in) to 2740m (9ft), providing an overall length of 4460mm(14ft 8in). The five-door hatchback, 'its lines as aggressive as a sports car,' with flared rear wheel arches, was aerodynamically refined in a way that imbued it with a very real sense of movement even when stationary.

Security Card Entry

External protrusions were accordingly kept to a minimum. For instance, the doors were opened by the use of a credit card-sized card rendering conventional handles unnecessary. Flush-fitting prismatic mirrors were adopted for the same reason.

Left: I.DE.A's adventurous idea for a smaller-scale multi-purpose vehicle, which is a growth area of the market, the Fiat Bravo-based Vuscia. The roof-mounted solar panels are used to power electric fans to keep the interior cool.

Below: An artist's impression of the Vuscia's rear which features an all-important tailgate. Note the absence of conventional door handles; instead for aerodynamic considerations, a credit card-sized 'key' is used.

The interior space was used to maximum effect with a potential owner being able to choose seating options. With all seats in place it was possible to accommodate six people in three rows of two, or to opt for two rows of seats for four individuals together with luggage space. Alternatively one row of seats allowed for even more room so that bulky items such as bicycles could be easily carried.

Solar Panels

A novel feature was that the vehicle's interior temperature was maintained at a comfortable level by the presence of fans powered by roof-mounted solar panels.

And the Vuscia name? That came from I.DE.A's Genova-born president Mantegezza. It means 'Sirs' in a local dialect, which the company says 'emphasises the car's highly spacious passenger compartment'. Presumably this does not exclude any ladies from also being carried!

Below: Although six people can be accommodated, this can be tailored to the type of load being carried. It has meant extending the Bravo's platform.

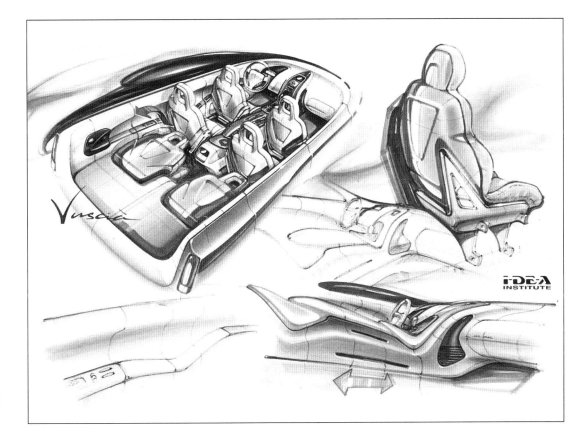

Peugeot Touareg 1996

Peugeot has been in the vanguard of creating electrically powered vehicles and its newest concept car, the four-wheel-drive Touareg unveiled at the 1996 Paris Motor Show, also used this power source.

The company described the Touareg and its Asphalte stablemate as follows: 'Relying on their sense of fun as much as their know-how, the Peugeot engineers and stylists have projected this philosophy into the future . . . Both cars are visually evocative but also lend substance to Peugeot's innovative abilities in the areas of electric power and chassis design.' So now you know!

The wedge-shaped Asphalte was an open two-seater sports car with a conventional petrol engine, but Touareg was visually and mechanically much more adventurous.

The nomadic Touareg tribe live in the sands of the Sahara Desert and Peugeot's futuristic off-road vehicle that borrows their name looks as though it would be equally at home in such terrain.

Below: The Touareg, at home in the sand dunes as well as on roads, was an emissions-conscious petrol/electric hybrid, an area in which Peugeot has established long-standing expertise.

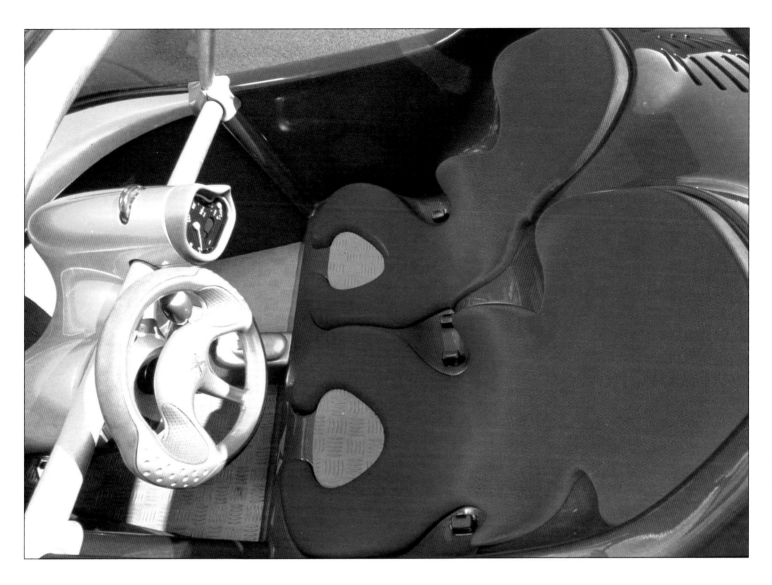

Beach Buggy

Its visual inspiration was the American Volkswagen Beetle-based Beach Buggy of the 1960s. These employed chunky glass-fibre bodywork, but Peugeot's fun car was built up around a single strong, but costly, carbon-fibre shell.

Look, No Doors!

The two-seater, with its red moulded seats, was deliberately made doorless. The occupants could simply jump in and drive off in

complete silence in a vehicle that eliminated harmful exhaust emissions. Top speed was about 112km/h (70mph), with 50km/h (31mph) reached in just five seconds and 80km/h (50mph) coming up in nine.

The Touareg was powered by an SA electric motor mounted in the centre of the vehicle behind the seats. Power was provided by a single block nickel/metal hydride battery and the drive system was similar to that used on the electrically powered version of the 106 hatchback that Peugeot introduced in 1995.

The power pack supplied the motor with 185 volts and maximum current of 250 amps. It produced a maximum output of 35.5 kilowatts although this could be temporarily boosted to 46.5 by the use of an on-board generator. This was driven by a small petrol engine that could also be used to extend the vehicle's range to a more practical 300km (186 miles).

Steering was power-assisted while disc brakes were fitted. Suspension was by all-round double wishbones and the 457mm (18in) wide wheels were specially designed by

Above: The fun element of the Touareg is reinforced by its colourful livery although weather protection is negligible. Consequently the interior is designed to be hosed down. Even the instrumentation is waterproof!

Michelin so that the colour-coordinated hub and tyre appeared to be made from the same material.

A vehicle such as this, built to be driven across country, gets dirty. No problem. Both the exterior and the interior, including the instruments, were designed to withstand a thorough hosing down!

Alfa Romeo Nuvola 1996

The Nuvola was a four-wheel-drive concept car with its lines firmly rooted in the sports Alfa Romeos of the 1930s. But it would be doing this stunning design an injustice to regard it as a mere pastiche, because its curvaceous lines possessed a vitality that is quintessentially late-20th century.

The Nuvola was the work of Walter de Silva, who was responsible for the styling of Alfa Romeo's acclaimed GTV/Spider, and is very much more than a visually impressive concept. It was also an attempt by the company to evaluate the feasibility of producing a space-frame platform that would allow bespoke coachbuilders to provide a variety of body styles, just as they had done between the wars.

This latter-day strategy would mean that Alfa Romeo could swiftly respond to changing market requirements and provide niche sector cars at reasonable cost.

Sketchy Start

Work on the Nuvola began in February 1996 and was completed in time for it to be unveiled at the Paris Motor Show eight months later. The original sketch was undertaken by de Silva and his ideas were transformed by Wolfgang Egger, a young German stylist, and his Italian assistant, Filippo Perini.

Power came from a twin-turbocharged 2.5 litre V6 engine, that is destined to appear in the four-wheel-drive version of Alfa Romeo's 166. In the Nuvola it was longitudinally, rather than transversely, mounted and coupled to a six-speed gearbox. The all-independent suspension was by double wishbones.

If these mechanicals were relatively conventional, the

Above: The Nuvola's headlights and side lamps are deeply recessed as in the manner of Alfa Romeo's gorgeous GTV. also styled by Walter de Silva. The Alfa Romeo radiator grille also reverts to its 1950s appearance. It incorporates both old and new themes that are to be found throughout the car.

Left: Spiritual 1930s lines refined for the 21st century. The car abounds with subtleties such as wheels that are flush with the bodywork. which will also feature on Alfa Romeo's new 166 saloon. For aerodynamic reasons. the window glass is almost level with the body sides.

coupé bodywork was not. Its pre-war spirit was underlined by the use of big 457mm (18in) wheels. At the front the traditional Alfa Romeo grille was flanked by twin headlights and indicators recessed into the separate wings in the manner of de Silva's Spider. At the rear were state-of-the-art light-emitting diode lamps.

The cockpit revealed strong nostalgic echoes of the original, but also incorporated modern elements based on that of the GTV/ Spider.

When the Nuvola made its Paris debut there was excited speculation that it might preface a prestigious coupé. Industry observers pointed out that the GTV's lines were anticipated by Alfa Romeo's Proteo four-wheel-drive concept car that appeared at the 1991 Geneva Show, just three years before the definitive model . . .

Racing Hero

But why Nuvola? The name derives from Italy's greatest ever racing driver, Tazio Nuvolari, who scored some of his most memorable victories at the wheel of an Alfa Romeo. Originally the car was to have been called the Tazio, but the town of Modena, which was Nuvolari's birthplace, objected, so Nuvola was chosen as a compromise.

Above: The Nuvola looks good from any angle. Bumpers contained within the body shell contribute to the clean lines. Rear lights are light-emitting diodes.

Below: Tradition abounds in the bare metal and leather-clad cockpit.

Mercedes-Benz F200 1996

Mercedes-Benz displayed, at the 1996 Paris Motor Show, its F200 coupé as its vision of the luxury car of the 21st century. As such it bristled with stylistic and electronic refinements. Of these, the most radical was 'drive-by-wire' controls which threatened to make the steering wheel a thing of the past.

This futuristic coupé therefore lacked a 'wheel and pedals. Instead, steering, braking and acceleration were controlled by a pair of ergonomically designed aircraft-style joysticks. One was traditionally positioned in the centre console and the other in the door recess.

The pioneering control system, which was coupled to the car's fully active suspension system, dispensed with traditional hydraulic and mechanical linkages. Instead the driver's commands were transmitted electronically by advanced computerized 'drive-by-wire' technology.

Joysticks

The car was steered by the driver moving the joysticks to the left or right, while alternative forward and backward movements controlled acceleration and braking.

Elimination of the steering wheel, steering column and pedals not only reduced the risk of injury to occupants in the event of a frontal collision, but also allowed for a more comfortable seating position for the cosseted driver.

Below: The F200's hydraulically-operated, scissor-type doors are activated as the driver approaches the car. As a result access is a great improvement on the more conventional hinged-type.

Significantly this arrangement could end the need for separate left- and right-hand-drive vehicles. The F200 could be driven from either front seat with all controls and the advanced digital driver display capable of being switched from one side to the other electronically, even when the car was on the move!

Video Eyes

The familiar rear-view mirror was also a thing of the past. Instead video cameras kept a watchful eye on approaching traffic and the images were displayed on a video screen which was located in the centre of the dashboard.

To increase driver comfort, the glass roof could be lightened or darkened, depending on weather conditions, at the touch of a button. This was possible as a result of its laminar construction in which conductive polymers sandwiched between the glass layers reacted to a small electric current.

Externally the F200's nose, radiator grille and headlights anticipated the company's S-Class cars expected for 1998.

There were no door handles; entry was gained by the use of a radio-controlled magnetic card that opened the doors as the driver approached the vehicle. These were hydraulically activated and of the upward-opening scissor type which ensured that there was plenty of room for entry.

Back at the turn of the century the Mercedes was the most influential car of its day. Will the 200's joystick controls make a similar impact on its latter-day contemporaries?

Above: While the boot lid looks conventional enough, its rises vertically when opened to permit ease of loading.

Below: Where's the wheel? Steering is achieved by use of one lever, in the usual 'gear' position to the right of the driver, and its door-located opposite number.

Citroën Berlingo Berline Bulle 1996

The diminutive bubble car was all the rage in the 1950s, but this latterday Berline Bulle, which means Bubble Saloon, was a very different concept. Its interior was, by contrast, positively palatial and conceived by Citroën as a halfway house between a saloon and an MPV (Multi-Purpose Vehicle).

Introduced at the 1996 Paris Motor Show, the Bulle was one of a trio of concept cars based on Citroën's new Berlingo van. Like its Coupé de Plage and Grand Large stablemates, it was created in-house but each vehicle was the work of a separate design team.

At the Crossroads

Built by Hurliez of Turin, the car was aimed at young families and designed to satisfy its owner's professional and personal requirements. It was a distinctive vehicle that, in Citroën's words, 'stands at the crossroads between a saloon and a people carrier.'

With a 2700mm (8ft 10in) wheelbase shared by the other concept vehicles, the Bulle, with a height of 1700mm (5ft 6in), was a lofty saloon. Its front, notably the bonnet and wings, were clearly related to its Berlingo parent although the headlight treatment noticeably differed. But from there on it took on its own very individual stylistic character.

Hubble, Bubble . . .

Oval forms were extensively used both in and outside the car, hence the Bubble name.

Below: Lightening the load, the Bubble is a car-cum-Multi Purpose Vehicle.

This roomy saloon also incorporated a large curved hatchback which improved luggage accessibility.

Interestingly the curved door lines echoed those of Citroën's prototype 2CV of 1939 which lost them when this legendary model entered production in 1948. They certainly helped to imbue the Bubble with its own utterly distinctive persona.

Citroën wanted the interior to be what it called a living area. Soft colours, such as grey and pale yellow, were deliberately used to 'place the accent on organic, gentle and reassuring shapes.'

With the emphasis also firmly placed on space, the broad back seat, which curved slightly inwards, was wide enough to seat three people

comfortably. Unusually the front seats were upholstered on both sides to make the interior more pleasant and inviting for the rear passengers.

The Berlingo van was diesel powered but the Bubble used Citroën's 103bhp, four-cylinder, 1.8 litre car engine similar to that used in the Xantia saloon.

Above: As the emphasis is on interior space, the Bubble's wheels are relatively small in proportion to its body.

Art Blakeslee, who is head of Citroën design, has said that he is not interested in concepts that do not become realities, and predicted that any of the trio could be developed for production within two years.

He will no doubt be studying consumer responses to all three projects, following their introduction at Paris and later at the British Motor Show. Who knows, we may be looking at a consumer friendly Citroën that takes over the mantle from the long-running 2CV in terms of individuality and flair?

Left: Three people can be carried in comfort, with plenty of leg room. The upholstery is rather traditional.

Concept 2096 1996

A concept car that anticipated a quantum leap forward to the year 2096 appeared at the 1996 British Motor Show which was held in the industry's centenary year. It bristled with initiatives of which the most radical was the absence of a driver in the accepted sense.

Below: Although it has the appearance of a slow moving mollusc, Concept 2096 was designed to slide along using a revolutionary, and yet unknown, 'slug drive' which dispensed with wheels.

Commissioned by the industry body, the Society of Motor Manufacturers and Traders, and featured on its stand, Concept 2096 looked more like a crustacean than a motor car.

It was conceived by Coventry University. The SMMT's brief was to use its flair and imagination to design a vehicle for the year 2096.

Initial work was allotted to final-year students at the university under the guidance of senior lecturer in design, Simon Saunders, and Samantha Porter, his opposite number in ergonomics. Further work was undertaken in Coventry by Geoff Matthews Design who also produced the full-size clay model.

In designing the vehicle, its creators' recognized that landmasses and local geography would probably be unchanged, and this factor also applied to the road structure. Having said that, they believed that motorways and other main and trunk roads could increase their capacity by as much as 50 per cent.

The reasoning was that all vehicles would be controlled by a road-management system and not physically driven by the individual user.

Slug Drive

Concept 2096 was designed to be powered by electric motors. These could be recharged while the car was on the move – perhaps from roadside senders in much the same way that a train receives current.

But there were no wheels, with propulsion, suspension, steering and braking all the responsibility of a mysterious, malleable, muscular material that does not yet exist. Perversely, its creators christened it slug drive.

The owner would enter the destination and preferred route into the onboard computer and it would do the rest. The navigation system could be geared for speeds of up to 483km/h (300mph) and accelerate or slow the car as and when required.

All such vehicles would travel in close proximity to one another under computer control to use valuable road space most efficiently.

Above: Not only would the car of the far distant future lack road wheels, there would also be no driver. Electric motors would rely on roadside sensors firing energy waves as the vehicles shot past. Speed would be computer-regulated which, hopefully, would see the end of traffic jams!

Colour Sense

The car was painted in so-called Smart colours by automotive paint manufacturer PPG. In open country it would change colour so that it would blend in with the natural environment. But on entering more urban surroundings it would alter to become more visible and so increase levels of personal safety; yet another innovative attribute of a truly remarkable vehicle.

Pininfarina Eta Beta 1996

One of the latest generation of petrol/electric hybrids, Eta Beta was distinguished by an expanding interior. Essentially a two-seater, when the boot was telescopically enlarged, it became possible to accommodate four occupants.

It was back in the 1970s that Italy's National Research Council launched its energy programme and chose Pininfarina as technical partner. This collaboration produced a number of aerodynamically refined electrically powered concept vehicles of which Eta Beta was the most recent.

Outwardly it was a one-box concept that concealed an aluminium space frame to which aluminium doors, bonnet and boot tail were anchored. The remainder of the body panels were made of a recyclable lightweight plastic.

Remote-Control Doors

Doors were of the gull-wing type and ingeniously constructed to take up the minimum amount of side movement. They had no handles and were opened by a remote-control servo mechanism.

It was possible, through a simple operation, to lengthen the rear overhang by 200mm (7.9in) to create three different versions of Eta Beta. It could be a 3120mm (10ft 3in) long two-plus-two-seater mini city car with a short tail. For intercity journeys, lengthened to 3320mm (10ft 11in), it

Below: Eta Beta's gull-wing doors were specially designed to take up very little space when opened.

became a long-tailed four-seater or, alternatively, an out of town vehicle for two which could also carry luggage.

The two propulsion units operated the front and rear wheels independently. The front ones were driven by a Fiat Cinquecento-derived 1108cc engine with its power output raised from 56 to 61bhp.

Two 12.5 kilowatt electric motors, developed by Rome University, were fitted inside each rear wheel which eliminated the need for transmission.

Messages from the accelerator and brake were fed to a microcomputer which conveyed signals to the motors via two electronic two-way converters.

Below: The tail can be lengthened to provide space for passengers or luggage.

Above: Pininfarina opted for a one-box configuration to maximize the interior space. Underneath the recyclable plastic panels is an aluminium spaceframe, making it a very easy vehicle to dismantle. Front wheels are petrol-driven and the rears electric.

Maintenance Free

The all-important maintenance-free batteries contained no liquid acid and were of the VRLA type. These Valve Regulated Lead Acid units were chosen because they eliminated the risk of spillage, which meant that they could be placed anywhere in the car.

Like other vehicles of this type, their charging took place during braking. When this occurred, the electric motors functioned as dynamos with power being conveyed to the batteries by the converters.

The driver would be responsible for selecting the propulsion mode most appropriate to the car's environment. In towns and cities, when operating on environmentally friendly electric power, Eta Beta had a range of about 40km (25 miles). But longer journeys could be undertaken using the economical petrol engine with distance, as with a conventional car, only limited by the contents of the fuel tank.

Mini ACV 30 1997

The AVC 30 made a surprise appearance in January 1997 to celebrate the fact that it was 30 years to the month since a Mini Cooper S had swept to victory in the 1967 Monte Carlo Rally.

An aborted styling concept, its ACV initials stood for Anniversary Concept Vehicle. Although discovered in the Munich styling studios of Rover's BMW owner, it was a joint British/German design.

It was spotted there by Tom Purves, previously managing director of BMW's British operations and currently Rover's sales and marketing director. He immediately recognized its potential value in the company's planned celebrations to commemorate the Mini's Monte Carlo win, the third and final occasion on which the model had triumphed in the event.

Spirit of the Original

In the ACV 30, the stylist succeeded in creating body lines that, while looking very much of a 21st century concept, nevertheless retained the spirit of the original. Finished in red, it also featured the white roof that instantly recalled the livery of the more potent Cooper variant. The battery of fog lamps also struck an appropriately nostalgic note.

The new Mini is due to appear in the year 2000 and will stick with the driven front wheels that made the original such a trend setter back in 1959. By contrast, the ACV 30 was a mid-engined, rear-drive vehicle and, as such, only had two seats. The production model will have four. This is because its front and rear subframes were courtesy of Rover's MGF sports car with power being provided by a 1.8 litre K-Series engine.

Below and right: Finished in the original red and white livery of the British Motor Corporation's Competitions Department, ACV 30 received a favourable response when it appeared in January 1997.

These were mounted in an aluminium space frame chassis while the body was of hand-beaten alloy. Unlike the production Mini, it incorporated a hatchback.

Memories are Made of This

Badged a Mini Cooper S, the rallying theme was continued in the interior which was furnished with competition seats and safety harnesses. Memories of the original Mini Cooper were to be found in the circular instrument panel positioned in the centre of the dashboard.

Rover has not revealed ACV 30's dimensions but says that it is about the same size as a Peugeot 106 which has an overall length of 3720mm (12ft 2in). What is undeniable is that it is somewhat larger than the production Mini which is just 3050mm (10ft) long.

This characteristic will be perpetuated in the new Mini, although Rover has declared that it will not be such a basic vehicle as the original, but a more exclusive and expensive small car. To be built at Rover's Longbridge factory, this second generation Mini will be powered by a Chrysler-designed, South American-built 1.4 litre engine.

With such an impressive concept car having been created and then rejected, the finished product should really be worth waiting for!

Right: The interior had the minimum of creature comforts and was clearly geared to competition. The centrally-located instruments echoed those of the original car while the seats came complete with rallying harnesses.

Dodge Copperhead 1997

Chrysler maintained its tradition for producing outstanding concept cars when it unveiled the Dodge Copperhead sports car at the 1997 Detroit Motor Show.

Created, says the company, in the spirit of the Austin-Healey 3000 of the 1960s, it will inevitably be compared with the larger Dodge Viper that originally appeared as a concept car at the 1989 event.

Venomous Snake

The Viper was regarded as a latter-day version of the AC Cobra. The reptilian theme extends to Chrysler's newest creation because a copperhead is also a venomous snake, infamous for attacking its victims without warning.

'Copperhead will be the sports car of choice for those enthusiasts who like the lithe, aerodynamic treatment combined with a low centre of gravity' said K. Neil Walling, Chrysler Corporation's design director. 'We designed Copperhead to look fast by utilising minimum overhang and pushing the wheels out to the front and rear corners.'

The show car was finished in what the company described as Fire Orange Yellow. Although its open two-seater steel bodywork and rear-wheel drive recalled 1960s' British influences it was, nevertheless, thoroughly modern in execution.

Individual Styling

Distinctive frontal features included twin air scoops in place of a grille positioned below deep-set quadruple headlights. The bonnet was elongated while the front wing contained sculpted air scoops. A scaled-down rear dorsal fin provided a further element of individuality and flair.

Power came from Chrysler's new 2.7 litre, 220bhp, aluminium V6 engine, with twin overhead camshafts per bank, and drive was conventionally conveyed via a five-speed, close-ratio manual gearbox.

Suspension was all-independent with semi-trailing wishbones front and rear. Brakes were all-round anti-lock discs. The distinctive alloy wheels were larger at the rear than the front and appropriately shod with specially commissioned snakeskin-tread Goodyear tyres.

The interior complemented the exterior with bucket seats upholstered in a Deep Amethyst snakeskin-like leather finish. Although the tachometer was mounted directly in front of

Below: Copperhead's distinctive, if restrained, lines. Chrysler viewed the model as a spiritual successor to the big Austin Healey. Drive is thus traditional, to the rear wheels, and brakes are discs all-round.

the driver, additional gauges, heating, ventilation and radio cassette controls were mounted centrally. When viewed in its entirety the console and pod bore a likeness to the head of the copperhead snake.

It was one of five concept vehicles that Chrysler unveiled at Detroit. Copperhead's stablemates were Pronto, a five-door hatchback, the Jeep-like Icon and Dakar, and the massive and luxurious V12-engined Phaeton convertible.

Of these Dakar and Copperhead looked the most ready for production. If so, this visually impressive sports car could be on the road by the turn of the century.

Above: The driving compartment, or should it be snakepit? The central console and instrument pod bear an uncanny likeness to the head of a copperhead snake.

Below: The Copperhead's low ground clearance is readily apparent, and the wheels are purposefully positioned at the corners of the car with the minimum of overhang.

Index